# Unqualified

*L*OVE AND RELATIONSHIP
ADVICE FROM A CELEBRITY
WHO JUST WANTS TO HELP

# ANNA FARIS

*with Rachel Bertsche*

ONE PLACE. MANY STORIES

1

First published in Great Britain by
HQ, an imprint of HarperCollins*Publishers* Ltd 2017

Copyright © 2017 by Unqualified Media, LLC

The photograph on page TK is copyright © Lacey Terrell.
All other photographs in the interior are courtesy of the author.
Unqualified Media, LLC asserts the moral right to be
identified as the author of this work.
A catalogue record for this book is
available from the British Library.

ISBN: HB: 9780008239251
TPB: 9780008239213

MIX
Paper from
responsible sources
FSC
www.fsc.org    FSC™ C007454

This book is produced from independently certified FSC™ paper
to ensure responsible forest management.

For more information visit: www.harpercollins.co.uk/green

Printed and bound in Great Britain by
CPI Group (UK) Ltd, Croydon, CR0 4YY

Anna Faris is an actress, producer, and top-rated podcaster: Her podcast, *Anna Faris is Unqualified*, averages four million downloads a month. Faris currently stars on the CBS hit comedy *Mom* and has had memorable roles on *Entourage* and *Friends*. She will next star in MGM/Pantelion Film's remake of *Overboard* alongside Eugenio Derbez. Faris produced and starred in *The House Bunny* and *What's Your Number?*, and her additional films include the *Scary Movie* franchise, *Lost in Translation*, *The Dictator*, *Observe and Report*, *Brokeback Mountain*, *Just Friends*, *Smiley Face*, *Keanu*, and the *Cloudy With a Chance of Meatballs* franchise. A native of Washington State, she lives in Los Angeles with her family.

*To Chris.*

*Your wisdom and strength have made me a better person.*

# CONTENTS

# CONTENTS

# CONTENTS

# FORWARD

## By Chris Pratt

When I was asked to write the forward for *Unqualified*, Anna's memoir, I immediately said yes without even thinking about it. And boy did a lot happen between then and now.

So much.

Like . . . soooo much.

So. Allow me to start by asking some questions:

First and foremost: What is a forward? Like, you know? What is it? Is a forward an anecdote? Like that time Anna and I went to the Beverly Hills library and I told her it was the first time I'd ever been in a library and then she looked at me like I must be joking? And I pretended I was joking? And boy did we laugh. But I wasn't joking? Is that a forward?

I don't really read books all that much. I mean, I know how to read, as in sounding out words and phrases, sentences, and the like. I can spell, too! I'll stop now. I feel like I'm bragging. But let's just say books aren't really my specialty. Per se.

I do read a lot of screenplays.

May I paint you a forward in screenplay format?

Fade in.

Int. Bedroom. Night. Chris Pratt (early twenties, roguishly handsome) stares blankly at his phone. He blinks a couple of times.

**Chris:** Siri. How do you write a forward?

**Siri:** Searching: How to go right and forward.

**Chris:** NO, STUPID! Siri. What is the definition of forward?

**Siri:** Searching: What is the definition of forewarn?

**Chris:** NO! Siri! Give me FORWARD definition.

**Siri:** Searching: Give me forearm definition.

**Chris:** Umm . . . Yeah. Show me that.

Distracted, Chris begins watching forearm workout videos for several hours.

```
Fade out.


Credits roll.


Thunderous applause. Oscar nom
Best Short Film. #blessed
```

Okay . . . Back to it.

Crickets.

Stares at phone.

Literally googles the word *forward*.

Wow . . . Okay. So . . . it's actually spelled FOREWORD. With an *O* and an *E*. Who knew? Siri did. Of course. We've been through a lot, she and I.

Anyhow, lesson learned. Now, let's move FOREWORD and discuss someone else with whom I've been through a lot.

```
         My Foreword
        By Chris Pratt
```

Anna is an important part of my life and she always will be. She asked me to write this foreword. And I'm doing so because I love and respect her and told her I would.

She and I have a striking number of similarities.

We were both raised in Washington State, just twenty minutes from each other. (Coincidentally, we didn't meet until working together in LA.) I played football on her high school field, a fact I've pointed out every single time we've driven past that school in ten years, to which, every time, she reacts with a gracious amount of faux wonder, kind sweetheart. We're both actors who made it in Hollywood, being cast as intelligently played idiots: me, Andy Dwyer; her, Cindy Campbell. We both have scars on our left hands, the results of drunken accidents that left us with nerve damage. We each had dead-bug collections before meeting. And even though they're not the same, Linda Goodman, author of *Love Signs*, claims our astrological signs are the most compatible with each other.

But there are a few differences as well. For one: Anna is a voracious information collector. She reads, hears, watches, and retains an inordinate amount of stories—from podcasts and NPR pieces to *New Yorker* articles. She'll often pore over the newspaper while simultaneously watching a TV show and blow drying her hair. She reads the big five: *The New York Times*, *LA Times*, *The Seattle Times*, *The New Yorker*, and *The Economist*. Whereas I read "The Big 5" sporting goods ads, looking for good deals on guns and Rollerblades.

Anna is kind, possibly to a fault. I'm proud to say we each approach most human interactions with politeness, and patience when required. We're both well-known actors, and it's worth mentioning—fame can be a pain in the butt. But we're thick-skinned. And despite what it may seem, we'll be just fine regardless of what you think of us. She's been in the spotlight longer than me yet continues to be the voice of reason in uncomfortable situations regarding our lack of anonymity. When approached by fans and photographers, she smiles and shows kindness. As do I, although my annoyance and bubbling anger with paparazzi tend to be more thinly veiled.

Anna is graceful with strangers and fans because she is

actually wildly interested in every person she meets. She asks great questions. She communes with anybody and makes an instant connection with each person she meets, which lasts . . . a VERY SHORT TIME. Like a "goldfish, three seconds, turn around and you're strangers" kind of way? Almost like Dory from *Finding Nemo*? Or the movie *Memento*? And that person, that nameless, forgotten person, knowing full well the moment is over, still somehow walks away feeling charmed and deeper in love than before. That's just how intoxicating she is.

Being TV and film stars, we live a circus lifestyle, pulled this way and that by jobs, strangers, lives on the road, all in service of the crowd. I see it as a calling in terms of the platform I've been given and a job that keeps me from breaking my back doing construction. For Anna, acting is a passion. She simply loves it. More than maybe anyone I know. There are home videos of her playing made-up characters from as early as eight years old. She started younger than that and really hasn't stopped since. On set and off she is constantly slipping into character, often her go-to clown: the awful party girl you may have seen in *Just Friends* (perhaps the greatest supporting role in a comedy by anyone ever—no hyperbole), as well as many more with our son. She lives to entertain.

And finally, more than anything, Anna deserves this book. I can promise you it will be a great and interesting read. A face-first dive into the mind and person that I spent one amazing decade with, and will, for the rest of my life, amicably coparent a human. She is the amazing, effervescent, former short girl, theater nerd, camp counselor, crossing guard, headgear-wearing, feistmeister, character-playing Anna Kay Faris, the "I was such a late bloomer I had to actually learn social skills to survive and developed wit to get by and then turned hot later" fan of *Real Housewives*, good times, extravagance, prudence, herself, her family, podcasts, books, white guilt, neurosis, great foods, repeated deep musical moments, mornings with the newspaper, small bites, feminism, and more.

And in all the years we were together, I don't think I smelled her farts once. They're probably not too bad.

Enjoy.

# Introduction

## *I Rote a Book!*

'm not qualified to write a book.

I might as well have woken up one morning and thought, *What can I do today that I have no experience doing, that I'm sure to make an ass out of myself while doing, and that will test a population's patience with my mental ability? Rite a book!* So I called my agent and got a book deal. Bingo, bango! Anyone can do this!

Truthfully, though, I'm terrified. I should have done a better job of thinking this through. You know how the biggest decisions in your life never appear as the lightbulb flashes you see in cartoons but instead germinate in the deepest crevasse in your brain and slowly take root until suddenly a blossom emerges in the forefront? That's pretty much what writing a book was for me. An idea I toyed with now and then, which eventually became more *now* than *then*, and suddenly I was pursuing literary agents and, before I had a chance to come to my senses, I was documenting my life (or at least my life in relationships) in writing.

As my mom keeps reminding me, I do have a degree in English from the University of Washington, a school that after five long, hard years taught me that I am unpleasant to be around after smoking weed out of a four-foot bong. But I don't think anyone, in my seventeen years of living in Hollywood, has ever actually asked me about my education. That's kind of the beauty (or horror?) of LA. No one gives a shit about any credit outside "the industry." So writing a book seemed like a fun, exploratory journey into the literary world, and a nice way to flex those English-major muscles.

But now the train has left the station and I feel as though I'm bound to disappoint many people in my life, including you, dear reader. I'm an actor, and have been since I was nine, so I should point out that I have been hiding behind characters and other people's words for a long time. There is always an out. Writing a book and putting my own words into the world is terrifying in the very way that performing in front of a camera will never be. In 2011, I naively and arrogantly agreed to be the subject of a profile in the *New Yorker*. It was written over the course of six months and when the fact-checker called me a few weeks before publication to read my own words back to me—words that I had spoken and completely forgotten—I knew I had to leave the country for good. My own vanity was about to destroy all I had worked for in Hollywood. Ultimately that didn't happen, but I did have to make a couple of apologetic phone calls.

Other small points of concern: I haven't used a computer properly ever, in my entire life. When you have a job where you make faces and say other people's words, you don't have to learn technology. Sometimes you don't even have to learn how to dress yourself, 'cause nice Lara is there to zip you up. So anyone at your neighborhood nursing home is more qualified to be punching these little buttons on this here keypad.

In fact, I think I might even have a typo in the title of this chapter.

Also, I don't know why I can't nap. I know that's not related, but it sort of is in that I want you to know *everything* about me, dear reader. You and I will be best friends after all this is over. I would like it if you would send me your autobiography, too.

Oh, and I'm really bad at social media. Why do I need to record everything online? Can't I just keep it in my brain? But I'm told that it's necessary to sell a book these days.

So, just so we understand each other, I don't know what the fuck I'm doing.

That's never stopped me before, though. Actually, that's not true. Until I was nineteen, I thought I was supposed to know everything. I didn't, obviously, but I accepted that there was a universal understanding that we all faked it, and the polite thing to do was quietly continue the charade. I knew to lay low and keep quiet so I wouldn't get made fun of. Then one day during my sophomore year at UW, I was sitting in the back of Intro to Something (Psychology? Sociology? I can't remember. I was miserable at the beginning of college. I sat in the back of giant lecture halls writing letters to Dustin, the "just a friend" I was in love with, who was studying abroad in Spain), when this good-looking fraternity guy raised his hand. I don't know what the professor was even talking about, just that the dude with his hand up said, "I don't know what that means." I remember a record scratch in my head: *Somebody just confessed they didn't know something?* There was so much bluster—everyone was always pretending they had all the answers. So it came as a shock to me that it was okay for someone—especially a hot frat type—to say, "Yeah, I don't know what you're talking about. Maybe you're all going to think I'm stupid, and maybe I am, but I don't understand."

There's liberation in admitting you don't know what you're doing. For me, it took years of comedy acting to get there. When you're shooting a film like *Scary Movie* you have to constantly confess that you have no idea if something is going to work, and it turns out it feels good to say, "I don't know how to do this."

So let me say it again: I have zero qualifications, and no one should be listening to me.

And yet, I want to help you with your love life. I do. I have advice to share—who you should date, who you absolutely shouldn't—and some cautionary tales, too. Plus, I'm fascinated by other people's relationships. In fact, I'm fascinated by other people's lives. What they ate for dinner, who they slept with last night; it's all equally interesting to me. And while I don't like to butt in, I do love to offer helpful, if sometimes unsolicited, wisdom. (That's butting in, isn't it? I'm the worst. I'm a horrible person.)

I've been doling out romantic advice my whole life. Most recently, and most publicly, on *Anna Faris Is Unqualified*, the podcast I cohost with my friend Sim Sarna, but my penchant for digging into other people's personal lives started decades ago. When I was eleven, my mom's friend came over to our house, sobbing. She was ranting about how awful her husband was, and I eavesdropped until I couldn't stand it anymore. "You have to leave him!" I butted in. She had two kids, but who cared? Kids, shmids. I was passionate about this. It was the only logical solution. She could run away and start a new life! She should totally leave him! Why didn't she just leave him?! It would be so easy! JUST LEAVE HIM!! When she didn't—because, of course she didn't, because life is complicated—I was profoundly disappointed.

My craving for a relationship of my own started before I played therapist to my mother's friend. For as long as I can remember, I wanted a boyfriend so, so badly. My mother, a ferocious feminist, couldn't stand how boy crazy I was. She hated *Pretty Woman* and didn't let me watch *Grease* because she disapproved of how Sandy changed herself for Danny in the end. She was adamant that I never be dependent on a man, and it created a massive inner conflict in me. I knew I wasn't supposed to long for a boyfriend as much as I did, which just made me want one more. I'd stay up late reading Sweet Valley High books, and even though I knew they were kind of stupid, I got off on the drama. The idea of boys fighting over me made me dizzy, probably because no one ever did. I bribed Jason Sprott, the fastest boy in the third grade, with ice cream just to get him to talk to me.

In the absence of a relationship of my own, I lived through other people's. I read Dear Abby and listened to Dr. Joyce Brothers and watched Sally Jesse Raphael. I did theater work around Seattle and was riveted when the lead actress flirted with the hot set dude. I wanted so intensely to be grown up, because to me, the defining feature of adulthood was getting to be in love.

When I was seventeen, I started dating my first official boyfriend, Chad Burke. He was unbelievably good-looking, but also, shall we say, "dark." Chad was popular, thanks to his looks, but he was also cynical and angry and would sneak out at night to write Rage Against the Machine lyrics on the telephone poles in our town. I couldn't believe that someone that hot would like me, and I was young, so I would have done anything for him. We went out for a year, and, like Felicity, I followed him to college. Two weeks after the school year began I would call his fraternity and he wouldn't come to the phone. I got drunk and went to his frat house and they wouldn't let me see him. Eventually we ran into each other and Chad told me he was dumping me. Clearly, I didn't have as much of a handle on the whole dating thing as I thought I did.

After Chad, I went from one relationship to the next. Because I was constantly trying to make a bad thing work, I was a serial monogamist, and I'm embarrassed to admit that it used to take meeting another person for me to realize that *Oh, this relationship might not be working.* I've had my share of romantic troubles, and what has continually provided me with comfort is the knowledge that millions of people out there have been through what I've been through. Heartbreak and rejection are communal. Love is life's greatest mystery and wildest adventure.

God, that's so fucking corny.

I started a relationship podcast because, to me, giving advice and hearing other people's stories is better than therapy. Not that I'm in therapy. I probably should be, but I find it too frustrating to not know anything about the person I'm talking to. The two times I visited a therapist I found myself asking about them—"I don't see a ring on your finger. Are you divorced? That must have been hard. Tell me everything!"—and they politely but firmly deflect and steer the conversation back to me. Then I try to get them to tell me about their other patients, which they seem to think is against some sort of rule.

Hearing other people's problems is, in its own weird way, comforting. It's a relief to me that so many of the trials I've had, other people have, too. And while I may be unqualified, I'm not uninterested. I care and I listen and maybe I don't always give the best advice, but I really do try. I dig a lot. I have no problem asking anyone anything. I'll try to curb my own obnoxiousness by saying, "I know this is personal . . . ," but then I go in for the kill: "How did you and your husband meet?" or "Oh, you're online dating? How does that work? Ever get catfished?" Some people really respond to it. Other people really, really don't.

I know what you're thinking: That all sounds great for a podcast, where that girl who looks like Mena Suvari can take callers and have a conversation, but what's going on with this book? Well, apparently, after two years of hearing other people's stories, I've learned a few things. About myself, about dating, and about the commonality of lust and heartbreak and desire and rejection and giddiness. I've been reminded that whether you're in LA or Atlanta or Dubuque, your pride will be wounded after a breakup, you'll struggle to tell a friend when you can't stand her boyfriend, and when you're truly happy, you'll know it. I've learned that there are some universal truths: If your closest friends stop showing up to your barbecues, you're probably in a bad relationship. And if you opt for kindness over teasing, you're probably in a good one.

I've come a long way since that night in 1987 when I so cavalierly told a mom of two to up and leave her husband. I don't get a rush from encouraging breakups anymore. These days I'm more interested in bringing people together. In fact, just recently, a friend of mine was going through a bad breakup, and thank God I was there. She and her ex had had this incredibly passionate, whirlwind courtship—within two months of meeting they were planning the wedding. But then they broke up, which was not entirely surprising in a situation like that. Shortly afterward, my friend came over to my house and was so incredibly upset. The more I thought about it, the more I knew I had to intervene. There was still a lot of love there, I just knew it, so I asked my friend for her phone. "What are you going to say?" she asked.

Didn't she trust me?

"Just let me have your phone," I said. My text was simple: "Hey, it's Anna. I don't know what you're doing right now but will you come over?" He did, and they had a beautiful, romantic night. I was so proud of myself! I got them back together and all would be fine and, like I said, I knew there was love there. I knew it.

He ended up leaving two days later and she was devastated and I think maybe a little annoyed at me. So, yeah. It backfired.

Still, points for trying?

In this book, you'll find stories of my relationships, both the disastrous and the heartwarming. You'll meet childhood Anna (pronounced *Ah-na*, rhymes with *Donna*, even though everyone gets it wrong and I never correct them), armed with flannel shirts and menacing headgear, and adult Anna, with more flannel shirts but much better teeth. You'll get some advice, a few lists, and some childhood photos (I'm the short one).

Read. Have fun. And please purchase the sequel: *I Have No Idea What the Fuck I'm Talking About: The Motherhood Book.*

# The Fastest Boy
# in the Third Grade

Remember when you first spotted him sprinting across the playground, schooling the other boys in a heated game of tag? Or the moment you noticed him at his desk, brown spiky hair sticking up in all the right places?

He was the first boy to make you crave the male gaze; he made you wonder what it would be like to have a boyfriend; he inspired you to start a diary.

You've been there, dear reader, haven't you?

For me, that boy was Jason Sprott.

Jason Sprott was the fastest boy in the third grade. You know how in elementary school everyone is known by their first and last name? Jason Sprott was always, and only, Jason Sprott.

He had the most adorable freckles and a great smile and spiky brown hair that I couldn't resist. We were in the same class, but we were nowhere near each other on the social hierarchy. Jason was a sweet, confident kid who totally knew his own charm—the top of the social food chain. I had more of a C-level social status. It started when I moved to Edmonds, Washington—a suburb thirty minutes outside Seattle—when I was six. I went from a blue-collar community in Baltimore where everyone was friends and had barbecues and family get-togethers to this faux-upper-class neighborhood that felt incredibly superficial. I know that's counter to the perception of Seattle, but my brother and I both felt like it was different in Edmonds. When I say I'm from Seattle it always feels misleading—moving to Edmonds felt a little bit like moving to Anywhere, USA. It did not live up to the Seattle stereotype.

We arrived in Edmonds in the spring, and on my first day of first grade, my mom put me in a really dramatic sheepskin coat. When she buttoned me up that morning, all I could think was, *I cannot wear this to my first day of school.* I was six, and even then I knew this was not good. A six-year-old in sheepskin does not have the makings of social success.

Sure enough, the other kids completely mocked me. It stung, but it also planted the seed for a weird-clothing rebellion that emerged in middle school. During those years, I wore the most hideous sweater, Charlie Brown but in reverse: it had more of the dark color than the light, and it was totally disgusting, but I embraced it for its ugliness. That sweater was my early fuck-you to the mean girls and the popular kids and the mundane existence I thought Edmonds offered. Then, in ninth grade, I wore a Christmas tree skirt like a cape, which of course got me lots of suitors.

*Do I look stoned in fifth grade?*

Looking back over the years, I've always gotten a lot of strength from being the underdog, or what felt at the time like the underdog. Maybe that started with Jason Sprott. He had a twin brother, David, but unfortunately for David they weren't identical. All the girls had a crush on Jason.

We were in the same class. Jason sat in front, as did his girlfriend, Michelle. I preferred to sit in the back and stare at my crush and his little hair spikes. I recently found the diary I kept in third grade, with pages of scribbles about Jason Sprott. *I love Jason Sprott. I hate Jason Sprott. I love Jason Sprott. He smiled at me today. We were assigned our Greek gods and he was Eros, the god of love, and I was the unsexy Hera but he shot me with his arrow.*

One day, I was in the cafeteria and Jason was behind me in the lunch line. After buying my lunch, I spent the thirty-five cents I had left over on the ice milk dessert. Ice milk was imitation ice cream before frozen yogurt was a thing. I guess it was better for you, but to us third graders, it was all the same. At least, it was appealing enough to get Jason's attention.

"Man, I wish I could get an ice cream," I heard him say behind me.

"I'll buy you one!" I offered eagerly.

This transaction—my using my extra change to buy Jason Sprott ice cream, Jason Sprott letting me buy him ice cream—went on for a couple of weeks, until finally he said, "I'll go out with you, but you've got to know that I'm also going out with Michelle." He was a real class act: he told me about Michelle and was honest that he wanted us both. *Sounds good*, I thought. *I'll take what I can get!*

Michelle was supercool and popular and had a fountain in her house, which was a big deal. The next year, in fourth grade, I invited her over to my place, and she actually accepted and came to my home. That was a shock. My mom had just bought an inflatable boat from Costco. She blew it up, and Michelle and I put it on my bed and played whitewater rafting adventure. We were laughing and really getting into it, riding the make-believe waves and capsizing onto the bed. I'd never seen that side of her. I thought we were having so much fun. A week later, the popular girls all made fun of me because I liked to play boat.

But back in third grade, when my romance with Jason was

blossoming, Michelle and I didn't have much of a relation-ship. Shortly after I bought Jason that first ice cream, she came up to me and said, "I know you're going out with Jason too, and I just want you to know I'm cool with it." She walked away before I could even respond.

Jason and I didn't speak to each other during our court-ship. I mostly saw him during recess, when everyone played tag, and of course he never got caught, since he was such a fast runner. It was the hottest thing about him. But even at recess we were G-rated. There was a big moment on the playground when Amy Gray and Sean Bryant were going to have their first kiss and everyone crowded around them and they ex-changed the tiniest little peck. That was a pretty huge event— I remember it more than any actual education I got in third grade. The non-kiss was a monumental moment in my social education. But with Jason and me, there was no peck. There was just the lunchroom, where I continued to bribe him daily with ice milk. I knew, on some level, that I was buying this guy. I wasn't getting his attention on my own merit. Even at eight years old, I was a realist. So while it was exciting that he went out with me, it felt like what I imagine it feels like when you win the lottery but you only win, like, $5,000.

Still, I envisioned myself as the third-grade Seattle equiva-lent of a scrappy Boston fighter. All odds were against me—I shouldn't say that, because I'm a blond white American person—but when it came to Anna versus Michelle, there was no comparison in the eyes of the elementary schoolers. I was the short girl who wore a sheepskin coat to her first day of school; Michelle had a fountain in her house. That pretty much said it all, and yet there I was, sharing Jason with her. For the first time, when it came to social status, I was A-list-adjacent.

Jason dumped me a couple of weeks later. He confronted me at recess and said, "I don't think we should go out anymore, I'm just going out with Michelle." It was a stab to the heart. I was devastated. I had nothing to give him but my thirty-five cents and he didn't even want that anymore. Maybe Michelle got in his head. She was supersassy and played her cards right. I, on the other hand, was a true sugar mama.

So I did what any heartbroken eight-year-old would do: I went home, grabbed an orange from the fridge, wrote Jason's name on the peel in black marker, and threw it off the deck into the forest outside my house. When I was a kid, I wanted to live in the Yukon, so I spent a lot of time in that backyard forest relishing my loneliness. I was dying to live a more dramatic life than Edmonds offered, even then. And this weird ritual, which I deemed "the orange ceremony," seemed like a start. I don't know where I came up with it. I certainly didn't read a book that said to pick up an orange and write a boy's name on it in order to get over him, but I ended up doing it with a few different love interests. I must have thought it was profoundly symbolic: that by casting this fruit into the abyss, I would somehow rid myself of the hold these emotions had on me. Even at that age, it's so surprising the intensity of feelings you can have for somebody. I felt the need to be liked and the need to be popular, but I was tortured by that neediness, because I was also proud and wanted desperately to be confident and independent. I thought the ritual would help. I remember throwing the orange out there and thinking, *Now I am complete! Now I am over Jason Sprott!*

It didn't work; I was not released. The next day I went to school and saw Jason, and saw Michelle, and was just as devastated.

That episode began my long and complicated journey with the idea of closure. Basically, I don't believe in it. I believe in the concept; I get why people crave it, and I understand why I, even in third grade, sought it from the orange ceremony. It's frustrating to feel so powerless against your own feelings. But as an adult, I've learned that closure is unobtainable. I think it happens at death, maybe. But remembering the pain is a good thing, because all those experiences that you can't close the door on make you a more empathetic person, and that should be embraced.

I have a pattern—it takes meeting a new guy to help me get over the old one. In the case of Jason Sprott, it was another Jason. He was the newspaper boy, supercute and a little bit brooding. I left him sodas outside my house every day so he could have a drink while he was delivering papers. I was totally into bribing these guys. *What can I give him out of my fridge that will get his attention?* I think there are five pages in my diary that read: *I am so over Jason Sprott, I am totally into Jason Berry. He is soooooooooooooo hot and such a mystery!* But one day he didn't take the soda, and I think that was his way of saying, "No more, you sad girl."

Despite our tragic end, Jason Sprott will always be my first crush. We ended up going to different high schools, so I lost track of him after eighth grade. He has probably changed a lot in the past thirty years. But to me he'll forever be Jason Sprott: lover of running, subsidized ice cream, and spiky bangs.

# List to Live By:
# The Professions of
# Men You Should Not Date
# (I Broke My Own Rules)

**B**efore you read this, a caveat: I am attracted to all these types of people. And in large part, have dated them. Or married them.

## 1. MAGICIAN

The idea that someone gets off on tricking you is just fucked up. I dated a guy in college who loved scaring me. He would hide behind the door and pop out just as I entered a room. Of course it freaked me out, but then I'd get mad. He'd giggle and I just wanted to punch him so badly. I didn't, because I don't have strong fists. But magicians have that similar desire all the time. To be clear, I love the idea of magic and the beauty and artistry around it, but the desire to trick people and never let them in on how you pulled it off? That seems to me like a person who will never fully reveal himself to you. I don't mind magicians as people, but in the realm of dating, the tendency to trick is very confusing to me.

## 2. MUSICIAN

Here's my theory on musicians: when you have an audience of more than ten thousand people worshipping you, how do you go home to your partner at night and be like, "So how was your day?" There's got to be an intoxicating head rush when you look into a sea of fans and know that you could have sex with any of them, no matter their gender preference. After that, can you ever be satisfied with anything less? Plenty of musicians don't achieve that level of success, I know, but even unsuccessful musicians are *looking* for that kind of attention. People who follow their creative passions are fascinating but also complicated, and they all have a tricky combination of narcissism and insecurity. The one thing that keeps some actors in check is that the crew is not laughing at their dumb jokes. The key grip is checking his phone and rolling his eyes, and he just wants to go home at the end of the workday. When you ad lib a joke, the boom operator, who has undoubtedly worked with much bigger stars than you, is probably thinking, *What a narcissist*, and you feel that, and it's humbling. But being a musician on a large stage? How do you separate yourself from the rockstardomness of being a rock star? So don't date musicians, except maybe a classical one. Second-chair oboe. I would stay away from first chair. And *definitely* not a conductor.

## 3. DOCTOR

My experience dating doctors has been that they've pretty much been dicks. Also, I have never dated a doctor. Plus, I saw that Alec Baldwin and Nicole Kidman movie. What was it called? *Malice?* The one where she's complaining to her husband, played by Bill Pullman, that "I hate our new neighbor" but of course she's screwing him because he's got a total God complex. That seemed realistic enough.

## 4. ATHLETE

Not necessarily because they cheat, which I know is what you're thinking. But because if they're getting older or there's a new recruit or they have massive injuries, you have to spend a lot of time stroking their ego. "Honey, don't you worry about Brock. I'm sure he'll tear his ACL too." After a bad game, you have to be so emotionally supportive, and the exhaustion will just burn you out. Plus, during the season, what are they going to have left to give you?

## 5. CHEF

I know, it sounds like a good idea. They'll cook for you. I get it. That's what I call the Chef Trap. Don't fall for it. As someone who has dated a chef zero times, I can tell you that the culture of the kitchen might not translate to relationships. It's hot and incredibly stressful, and, as I know from experience watching *Hell's Kitchen*, temper is encouraged. If people have a hot temper at work, I just don't think they can avoid bringing it home. And he probably gets home at three thirty in the morning.

## 6. THERAPIST

I haven't been to much therapy at all. It terrifies me. Growing up, my parents were of the belief that if a person is in therapy, that was true validation that they had a mental illness. But in LA, you're the person with the mental illness if you're *not* in therapy. So I went once, and the therapist asked me where I see myself in ten years. "I'd like to live in Northern California in a house with a lot of land and plants and maybe an amphitheater to put on plays," I said.

He responded, "Do you realize that in that explanation you didn't mention your son once?" I wanted to throw something at him. *Um, that's why I want to go there, dick, to be with my son and give him everything I wanted as a kid. And would you ever say that to a man? Question his commitment to fatherhood because he focused on himself in therapy?* After that, I was therapyless for years because it made me so furious. If you date a therapist, I imagine their silent judgment at home, your therapist boyfriend dissecting the meaning underlying everything you say or do. And who wants to date someone who is going to be analyzing them all the time?

## 7. ACTOR

We all just need so much praise. I know I do, and male actors are the same way. Still, I can't help but be attracted to them.

And I know many men have actresses on their "don't date" list, too. Of my four serious relationships, two of the men—so, not a great percentage—told me their moms said they should never date an actress. Hearing it for the first time was jarring. After the second, it was like, *Is this really a thing?* I wasn't even successful yet. I was doing local Seattle theater, and I wasn't all that dramatic of a person. I just wanted men not to cheat on me.

Basically, the only profession you can or should date is a woodworker, or a guy who makes boats. Like Kevin Costner in *Message in a Bottle*. Someone who is brooding but carves wood all day, making something gorgeous with his hands while he ruminates on lost love, and finding new love, and stormy seas.

## *Ich Liebe Dich*

C had Burke was my first boyfriend. He was a junior, I was a senior and, as far as I was concerned, he was the hottest guy in our high school. So I couldn't believe it the night we kissed at a Stone Temple Pilots concert. Chad was incredibly angry—this is the guy who snuck out at night to write Rage Against the Machine lyrics on telephone poles—which turned out to be a theme in my life. I spent a long time feeling drawn to angry men.

Chad worshipped Steven Seagal. He looked like a high school version of the action star, with the low ponytail and everything. It was 1993, back when that was sexy. (Was it, though? Or was that just me?)

Chad was popular because he was good-looking, but not in the way well-liked people are popular. He would never have been elected the captain of a team or voted Most Likely to Succeed or anything like that. He was a cynical, bitter teenager, but looks can get you far in high school.

He was smart, too—although, can we talk for a minute

about how fucked-up our societal intelligence scale is? Why do we gauge smarts the way we do? I say this out of pride, because I took an intelligence test in high school that scored students on a level of 1 to 5 and I got a 2. The teacher told me my score and suggested that I should become a secretary and I was so pissed off. Not because secretaries are dumb—I'm sure most secretaries are plenty smarter than a 2 out of 5—but because being told what I "should" or "could" do, as if I was too stupid for anything else, was infuriating.

Similarly, I scored a 1060 out of 1600 on the SATs and I remember this guy in my grade asking me what I got, and after I told him he said, "Oh my God, I thought you were so much smarter than that."

"I know," I said. "I thought I was, too!"

Thank God I had parents who believed in me, because I really took that secretary thing to heart, and if I didn't have a family who constantly encouraged me I certainly wouldn't have the confidence to write this book that I'm totally un-qualified to be writing.

But anyway, by *conventional* standards, Chad was smart.

One September evening in 1993 a group of seven or eight of us went to a Stone Temple Pilots concert. It was exhila-rating to be out with the cool kids. I was not in the popular crowd in high school, and while I mostly tried to stay under the radar, I found myself on the receiving end of mean girls or general mocking a decent amount. Being a theater kid wasn't looked highly upon in Edmonds. So for the concert, I told my mom I was staying the night at my friend Stephanie's, and instead I went to the concert with classmates I didn't usually hang out with. So there I was with this hot dude making advances on me, and it was a whirlwind of not just physical but mental intoxication. All I could think was, *This is the best night . . . Of. My. Life.* Chad and I made out, and despite the fact that we were completely stoned and smashed in a sea of sweaty fans and standing in front of our classmates—or maybe because of that—I thought it was completely magical. A couple of days later, when Chad asked me to be his girlfriend, I was overjoyed. He snuck over to my house in the middle of the night and put a big banner in my window that read ICH LIEBE DICH. That's "I love you" in German. He was a big German studies fan.

Chad and I got very passionate very quickly. We would look into each other's eyes and say that we would die without each other. One day my mom looked at me and said, "Anna, I've never seen you this happy before." I hadn't told my parents about Chad because I was too embarrassed. It was incredibly important to my mom that I wasn't boy obsessed, which was a hard standard to live up to as a teenager. And, of course, I *was* boy crazy, but instead of just embracing that as a normal phase of my teen years, I was ashamed. I thought I shouldn't feel the way I did, so I never told her anything about boys—not Jason Sprott's ice milk or Jason Berry's sodas or anything.

But once my mom noticed that something was different, I admitted that I was dating someone, and that I really liked him. I showed her Chad's picture, and I remember her saying, "Oh, he's so handsome." It was gratifying to hear her say that, but I also thought, *Mom, you could not have said anything worse because now I am diving in headfirst. If you are going to approve of this, I am so in.*

I was crazy for Chad. He was just so hot and angry, which were my only two requirements in a man back then, and I was in such disbelief that anyone so good-looking would like me that I would have done anything for him. If he had said, "I really, really, really want to have a threesome," I probably would have been like, "Great! With who? Where? The parking lot? Awesome!" He was the guy I lost my virginity to (more on that later) and my first love. It was that heady rush of young love that has no basis in logic at all. I really thought we were going to get married—he gave me a promise ring!—so when he decided to graduate a year early and enroll at the University of Washington, I followed him there.

Two weeks before college, Chad asked if I would mind if he joined a frat. I told him I didn't mind at all, even though I had no plans to be a part of the Greek system. The week that college started, I didn't hear anything from him for three days, even after repeated pages. (Yes, pages. Again, 1994.) So eventually I stalked him. (Yes, stalked.) I knew where all his classes were—and this was a huge school, like forty-five thousand undergrads—so I conveniently found myself outside one of the buildings at just the right time and "bumped" into Chad. He saw me and said, "Oh yeah, I've been meaning to tell you I want to see other people."

It was a blow. I must have known on some level—he hadn't communicated with me in a few days, which was a pretty strong indicator that something was off—but I was still devastated. So I did what any self-respecting reluctant ex-girlfriend would do, and continued to stalk him. Maybe it was more like borderline stalking. I showed up at his fraternity, and his frat brothers would say, "Chad's not here," and I'd gasp out between drunken sobs, "Why . . . isn't . . . he . . . here? Where . . . is . . . he?" Then they'd escort me back to my dorm and it was all very pathetic and dramatic in that way that only happens during college.

Four months later, in January, Chad moved into a probably illegal apartment next to a Korean restaurant, which smelled like kimchi had permeated the wallpaper. Soon after that, he called me in my dorm and told me he wanted me back. I did not pass go and ran directly into his waiting arms.

Within the week, I realized I'd lost all sense of myself for this douchebag of a person. But instead of being courageous that very day, I went home and wrote in my calendar that on March 14, I would break up with him. For whatever reason, that was the day I chose—two months away.

I stuck it out for those two months, even though everything about Chad drove me crazy by then. I would stare at his long, delicate, artistic fingers and feel a tug of annoyance. His pride at wearing Tevas, as though he were a river-rafting guide, made me cringe. So did his ponytail, and his cackling laugh, which was usually directed at someone less fortunate than he. One time he told me, after pointing out a Darwin fish sticker on the back of a car, that he "could have invented that." The worst grievance of all was his surprise at my decent acting skills in the idiotic Steven Seagal fan videos he made with his friends. But mostly, I was horrified by those fingers. Sometimes I worry that if I get dementia like my grandma (who, by the end of her life, talked exclusively about how her brother burned down the family farm when she was nine) I'll spend my life ranting about Chad's fingers. In that case, I like to think my family could make a solid case to the state for assisted suicide.

It turned out I needed those two months to realize that I hated more than what I liked about Chad, and to muster the confidence to put my first real relationship behind me. I needed to digest all of it before I really broke it off.

On March 14, I woke up and thought, *This is the day I have to have some pride.* I marched over to Chad's place and said, "I'm leaving you," and he didn't say anything. He just walked to his fridge, pounded a beer, threw it at a wall, and said, "You're going to be back here in a week." At that point, I knew that even if I did want to be back there in a week, which I kind of did, I couldn't ever return.

So that was the end of Chad Burke. Almost.

Ten years later, right before I married my ex-husband, I tracked Chad down—which was probably a sign that I shouldn't have been getting married in the first place. I called his mom, and when she picked up I was just like, "Hey, Mrs. Burke! You might not remember me but this is Anna . . . ," and she im-mediately said, "Oh, hi! I've been following your career. It's so great." The way she spoke to me, and her lack of surprise at hearing my voice, it was as if we'd chatted two days earlier. It was so strange. I told her I'd love to catch up with Chad and gave her my number. At the time I was in New Orleans shooting the movie *Waiting . . .* , and the next night, Chad called. It had been twenty-four hours since I'd reached out to his mother—enough time for me to come to my senses. My phone rang and all I could think was, *Oh fuck, what am I doing? Why am I reaching out to my ex when I'm about to get married?* I didn't pick up.

He called three more times. I had started this, I realized, so the polite thing to do was at least talk to him. We ended up on the phone for six hours. He lived in San Francisco, and he told me the most grotesque story about going to China and marrying a woman who was in love with someone else. It might not sound like a funny story but I laughed so hard, and remember thinking, *Okay, I made the right choice.*

In the end, that wasn't entirely the case, and that marriage ended in divorce. But the Chad Burke call was another in-stance of me reading a lot into the idea of closure. Chad was my first love, and we all romanticize our first loves. Especially as a teenager, when the emotions flood into your brain in a way that doesn't happen in your thirties. I do wonder, though, why we are always so tempted to revisit that first relationship. In the very best- case scenario we have someone begging for us back. "Oh my God, you're the one that got away," they might say. "I can't believe I fucked it up. Is there anything I can do to get you back?" But the reality is that that's not going to happen. And do you really want someone to say that anyway?

To be fair, hearing that the guy who treated you like crap might want you back, and realizing that you're over it—that you don't need them, and certainly don't want them, and are actually too good for them—would definitely feel empowering.

So, yeah. That would be kind of great.

# Unqualified Advice:
## Squad Goals?

**W**hen I was cast in *Scary Movie*, I called my friend and former college roommate, Claire, to tell her that I landed my first big role. She was thrilled. And then I told her that it was a spoof comedy, and, with a voice full of concern, she said, "But, Anna, you're not funny."

It wasn't mean; it was true.

"I know," I said. "I don't know what I'm going to do."

It's a very special kind of friend who can verbalize your insecurities in a way that is a show of support rather than a teardown. When Claire reminded me that I wasn't a comedian, she was saying, "Okay, how should we tackle this?" Not "Man, you're going to fuck this up."

I've never been the kind of gal who surrounds herself with female friends. I've never had that *Sex and the City* posse— I haven't met my ladies regularly for brunch or had a group that I just called "the girls." I always wanted that, but I never knew how to get it, so instead I clung to the man in my life at any given time.

But I do usually have two or three incredibly close girl-friends, and I am fiercely loyal to those people.

For a while, in my twenties, I thought it was cool to say that I was a guys' girl. I didn't realize until later how lame I sounded, bragging as though having a lot of girlfriends was a bad thing. Back then I thought that having the approval of my stoner guy friends was of great intellectual value, while friend-ships with beautiful blond sorority girls would be shameful, so I touted my male friends as if my association with them spoke to how cool I really was. But, like I said, that was lame. I was selling my own gender down the river, and I wasn't even get-ting any fulfillment from the relationships with those stoner dudes. The truth of why I didn't have girlfriends probably had nothing to do with my being a guys' girl and everything to do with the fact that I was angry and jealous and unduly proud of the guys I was hanging out with.

That said, I did have some precedent for shying away from packs of ladies. Growing up, I fell victim to plenty of mean girls. In fifth grade, for example, I was invited to a girl named Mandy's house for a slumber party. Mandy was one of the most popular girls in school, and I couldn't believe I was in-vited because I was not in her social circle at all. My mom was really skeptical, but I begged her to let me go. She did, and I joined Mandy and her two friends, Lindsey and Amy, and they made fun of me the whole time. "Let's play boat!" they said when I got there, which I knew was a reference to my ill-fated playdate with Michelle a year earlier. At one point the girls said we should all take a shower together, and they made me close my eyes and I could hear them laughing at my body. It was fifth grade, so I don't think they were especially developed or anything. Our bodies couldn't have looked that different from one another. I think I was simply the nerdy girl who liked to play imaginary games and they wanted someone to pick on. I'm sure they invited me to the party for just that reason. (It was so wild to me that my mom totally picked up on what was happening—she knew the party wasn't a good idea and that these were mean girls. I never told her about what happened, though, because I was too proud. I didn't want her to be right.) In high school, Mary Young and her crew had a running joke where they would sneak up on me and snap my bra strap. It may sound like a small thing, but when you're a quiet teenager trying to get through high school unnoticed, that kind of unwanted attention is rough. One day, I went to my locker and the words *fuck you, bitch* were written across it in permanent marker. It was humiliating. But it was also confusing—I didn't think I was worthy of that kind of hatred. I generally flew under the radar in school, or at least I tried to. Yes, I did some acting in local theater, and I was in a commercial. I played the chubby kid in a frozen yogurt ad, for which I was paid a $200 gift certificate to Safeway. (I wasn't really chubby, but I had a weird round face as a kid and the commercial was entirely close up. The script said: "Chubby girl: 'Mom, are you eating ice cream?'" and I remember one of the producers saying to my mom, "Oh, she's not chubby, we just call her that because she has a chubby face.") But at school I primarily focused on how to be as small as possible. The guiding question of my teenage years was simply, How do I survive this time in my life?

I did survive, ultimately. It was rough, and cool was never something I felt, so eventually I accepted my lack of girl-friends and left high school. But years later—twenty, to be exact—I returned.

After graduation, I kept in touch with very few people from high school. Aside from Chad Burke—with whom I lost contact after freshman year of college—there was only Meghan, who was a grade below me and is currently a writer in New York. She was, and is, wonderful and smart and funny, but I think the thing that initially kept us connected was that we both broke out of Edmonds. So when my ten-year high school reunion rolled around, it never even oc-curred to me to attend. Just before my twentieth, however, some girls from my grade reached out to my older brother on Facebook.

"They'd really like you to come," Bob told me over the phone. I didn't want to, quite honestly. Not because I'd have to revisit the mean girls, but because I didn't keep up with anybody. Was I really going to fly to Edmonds to attend a reunion of people I barely knew and who, a couple of decades earlier, had no interest in me?

Still, it seemed like I'd be sending a complicated message if I didn't go—I didn't want it to come off like I thought I was too good for Edmonds—so Chris and our son, Jack, and I took a weekend trip back home. It was 2014. *Guardians of the Galaxy* had just come out and Chris was at the beginning of megastardom. I told him that I didn't want to subject him to my reunion, which was true, but I also didn't want the story to be that "Anna showed up with Chris." We decided I'd attend alone and he'd pick me up at the end. All those years later, the idea that I would come in and command any type of narrative still made me anxious. High school reunions are strange that way. They tap into so much—who we were, who we've become, who we want to be, and how we want to be perceived. So while intellectually I knew that plenty had changed in those twenty years, once I stepped into the school, it didn't feel that way. I was still awkward and uncomfortable and without any good friends; and the mean girls were still huddled in the corner, and they still seemed pretty mean.

This is where you might be picturing Romy and Michele. You might think that I swooped in and wowed the crowd with how fabulous I'd become in the decades since graduation.

You would be wrong.

It's true that fame and success have given me more value to some people who otherwise might not want to talk to me. There were a couple of former classmates I chatted with who perhaps wouldn't have been interested if I hadn't "made it" in Hollywood. And, honestly, I was surprised, but pleased, by how little satisfaction I got from that. Because while that satisfaction might have been human, it might also have made me a giant asshole.

The truth of the evening was that there was no "I showed them!" I was not the belle of the ball. Mostly, I was snubbed. The same girls who were mean to me when I was eighteen were whispering about me at thirty-eight. But there was something almost comforting in that—not the talking about me so much as the simple knowledge that some things don't change. Mean girls stay mean. I was perversely happy about it.

There was one person at the reunion who I was looking forward to seeing. My old friend Matt. We had been close in high school. I'd had a big crush on him, and of course he knew it. At the reunion, we caught up and he introduced me to his stunning wife, who was lovely, and then he turned to me and said, "I just want to apologize for being so mean to you." I knew what he was talking about. Junior year, Matt recorded me talking shit about our mutual friend Jeff. Then he played it for Jeff, just to make me look like a bitch. (I have this theory that we all need to publicize the list of suspects who should be investigated in the event of our murder. If I turn up dead, definitely find out what Jeff was up to.) But when Matt apologized all those years later, it was insulting. Of course I remember how he betrayed me with that recording, and it definitely caused a clear shift in our friendship, but I'd been so excited to see him, and there was so much funny shit he could have referenced from our past instead. It had been twenty years. I was over it. Maybe.

Part of the reason you go to a high school reunion, I think, is to get confirmation that other people remember you as you remember yourself. That night, when former classmates said they recalled me being quiet in high school, it was such a relief, because that's what I remember, too. So Matt's apology didn't feel long overdue or make me feel in any way vindicated. It just stung. That's what he remembered?! I thought this was someone I had really connected with, and I'd been so eager to see him. The idea that I was reduced to this one moment where he treated me like shit was kind of humiliating. I have this image of Matt and his wife driving to the reunion together and him saying, "Yeah, I was really mean to Anna, so I'm going to apologize tonight," which I know might be said with the best intentions but just feels gross.

After that interaction, I was done. I'd been at the reunion for all of one hour, but it was long enough for me to feel like I was in high school again, and to be ready to get out. I mean, Green Day was pumping through the loudspeakers. Chris drove down and picked me up, as we'd planned, and it did feel a bit like the lion rescuing the lioness from the hyenas. It was amazing to watch the reaction as he came through the door. I still felt like headgear-wearing, awkward Anna Faris, but when Chris came in, he was all movie star. There was a collective gasp as he whisked me away and, yes, that was fairly satisfying, I guess. I'm human, after all.

It took me longer than it should have to realize just how important female relationships are in my life. That shift only happened fairly recently, maybe in the last three to five years. It takes vulnerability of spirit to open yourself up to other women in a way that isn't competitive, and that's especially hard in Hollywood, where competition is built into almost every interaction.

Female actresses don't get to work together very often, so we truly don't have a ton of face time with one another, though I do like to think that's changing. With guys—like Chris and Seth Rogan and James Franco—they're all buddies and do each other favors and appear in each other's projects. And of course plenty of women do that, too, but sometimes I'm envious of the communities that male actors can establish merely because there have been historically more roles for men in any given project, so they have more opportunities to forge relationships. I have it on my to-do list to host a monthly boozy brunch with a bunch of actresses and no agenda so we can just hang out. Right now, the only times we see one another are at these crazy high-pressure Hollywood events where you're all wearing gowns and one of you—not me, but the person I'm talking to—is nominated, so she's distracted and freaked out and in no mood to get into girl talk. Like Emma Stone or Jessica Chastain or Amy Adams, all those stunning women who I never see until the awards shows at which they are, rightly, being celebrated and I'm busy loading up on champagne-infused complimentary snacks.

But between filming a sitcom and recording a podcast and raising a five-year-old, I bump up against a lot of the same internal struggles that most working moms do. As much as I want to host my boozy brunch, making time for it in my schedule hasn't been a priority. I can hardly keep up with the friends I already have. My oldest pals constantly give me a hard time for being so bad at texting them back, but that's because I don't want to have a texty relationship. I want to spend an hour talking and getting into the good stuff. I don't have a lot of patience for small talk. I don't even like the phrase. Why would I want to engage in conversation that people deem small? But that means I don't text back or pick up a call until I have the time to devote to that person. Which often results in "Are you mad at me?" texts, which just make me want to put off a call even more, because I know the first twenty minutes will consist of apologies instead of conversation.

I've heard the suggestion that I don't need a tight group of girlfriends anyway, because your partner should be your best friend. But I've never bought that. The idea that your mate must be your best friend feels to me like an overused mantra that puts unnecessary pressure on your relationship. I really believe that your partner serves one purpose, and each friend serves another. There's the friend who you confess things to, and the friend with whom you do the listening. Or this is the person I talk to when I'm feeling lonely and sad, and this is the person I talk to about work shit, and this is the friend I'm still in touch with because we grew up together. To be honest, I think the notion of best friends in general is messed up. It puts so much pressure on any one person, when I truly believe it's okay to have intimacy with different people in different ways. That's why I'm so glad I never had bridesmaids. It seems like a tradition entirely engineered toward forcing you to rank your friends, and that really bothers me. It just shouldn't happen, at least not beyond grade school.

Today, I'm lucky to have a handful of women I count as confidantes. Allison Janney, my costar on *Mom*. My friend Alex, who I met when we worked on *The Hot Chick* together. Meghan, the friend who got out of Edmonds and writes in New York, and Kate, a dear childhood friend and neighbor who, on paper, I have nothing in common with anymore—at least not from an outsider's perspective—but who totally gets me because, history. Six months ago I called her and said,

"Kate! I was reading this article and I think I have this condition called prosopagnosia, where you are totally face blind and don't recognize people that you've seen before."

"Oh God, you totally have that," she said. "Remember that time at the park when you thought your mom was walking across the field and it was really that homeless guy?"

Confirming that I might actually have prosopagnosia, instead of just saying I was crazy, might be the kindest thing she ever did for me.

# Losing My Virginity,
# and Other Horrible
# Sexual Escapades

I had my first kiss when I was sixteen and lost my virginity when I was seventeen. It was a busy couple of years.

The kiss was during my junior year of high school. It was a Friday night and we had just finished a production of *You Can't Take It With You*, a Pulitzer Prize–winning play in which I played Essie Carmichael. It was a juicy part. Not the lead, but a good, meaty role that allowed me to show off my acting chops. (I love beef references, dear reader.) After our performance, some of the seniors in the cast rented a hotel room in downtown Seattle. I told my parents that I was spending the night at my friend Stephanie's (yes, Stephanie was also my alibi during the Stone Temple Pilots concert where Chad and I first hooked up—"staying at Stephanie's" was a recurring theme of my teenage years), but instead I went to the hotel room and got wasted. It was my first time being drunk, and Kyle, a senior, held my hair back while I vomited, which anybody who has ever been a drunk girl in high school knows is both disgusting and the epitome of romance all at the same time. After I was done puking, we crawled into a bed where Jeff (the same Jeff who I mentioned might murder me) was already passed out. He was lying on the right side of the bed, Kyle was in the middle, and I was on the left. I don't know how Kyle could stand kissing me after I vomited, but we made out a little bit and then he fingered me right there in that king-size hotel bed for three. (In hindsight, maybe Jeff is right to want to murder me.)

I had a minor crush on Kyle—he had a huge grin, big dimples, great hair. He was the kind of guy who seemed stoned all the time, but I don't think he actually was. The fact that he was able to look past my braces and stinky vomit breath and stick his tongue down my throat was a true gift, even if it did feel like there was a slug in my mouth and I had no idea what I was supposed to do. Aggressively kiss him back? Passively receive the kiss? I wasn't sure. (To be fair, I'm still not sure I know how to kiss properly. I always wonder if I'm doing it right. Even though I'm an actress and kiss people in movies all the time, you can't exactly ask, can you? And even though those are technically first kisses, I also think about the rush of a real first kiss and wish I could have that without all the teenage awkwardness.)

That night at the hotel was an evening of firsts: my first make-out session, my first finger bang, my first night in a king-size bed. I was in heaven. So much so that I couldn't wait to write all about it in my diary: *I made out and was penetrated! Life is grand!*

The next morning, I went home first thing because I was scheduled to take my driver's test. My parents—the sweet, supportive people they are—were raving about my performance in the play while all I could think was, *I hope they don't smell the vomit and cigarette smoke.*

Somehow, I passed my driver's test. It was a major twenty-four hours in my life. But the blissful high of making out and having a license was short-lived. A few days later, my mother found my diary. She read my recap of Kyle's finger-banging and thought it meant I lost my virginity, and she was furious.

Here's the thing about my mother . . . she wanted me to stay a virgin until I was married. She made that very clear. This always confused me, because my mom is not a religious person. If her views had been based on God or the Bible, I would have at least understood the root. But she was a steadfast feminist, so her message seemed complicated. I think it was instilled in her at an early age that, as a woman, your sexuality was a dangerous and powerful tool, which had to be used extremely carefully. It must have been complicated, because she and her sisters were, and are, unbelievably gorgeous women with incredible figures. Growing up, they were dirt-poor but were known as the local hotties, and each of them reacted very differently to the power that comes with being unbelievably attractive. And I'm not saying this just because she's my mom. She's really a knockout. I have these beautiful pictures of her framed in my kitchen, one taken when she was nineteen and the other when she was twenty-seven. At a far glance it looks like me, but when you get closer you see that she had everything that I don't: a seventies'

Playboy Bunny look—soft hair, high cheekbones, full lips. She must have really struggled with the complicated power of feeling beautiful and the desire to be desired and the guilt she felt toward anything sexual at all.

"Anna, you just don't know your own value," my mother said after she read my diary. I didn't get it. I was supposed to be an independent woman, but at the same time I wasn't supposed to do what I wanted with my body? It didn't make sense.

Needless to say, when my mom read about my night with Kyle, she was pissed—and I was, too. I was devastated that she would look at my private journal, and it was clear she didn't even understand what she had read. I didn't have sex that night, obviously, and it hurt me that my mom couldn't tell that I was really quite protective of my body—something I thought she should understand just by knowing me. Let's be honest, I could have had sex anytime I wanted, because I was a sixteen-year-old girl surrounded by sixteen-year-old boys, and sixteen-year-old boys just want to bone.

So I did what any teenager angry at her mother would do and threatened to move out. To Stephanie's house, of course.

A word about Stephanie: We became friends through drama class. I was a D+ on the social level, but she was a solid B. Not superglamorous but very well-liked; she was in drama, though, and that hurt her A. Where I went to high school, doing drama was sort of social suicide. Stephanie had an International Harvester Scout, an old car that was, once upon a time, an alternative to a Jeep. Hers was white and blue, and we used to drive around Edmonds in that truck listening to New Order and it was awesome. She also had a lot of independence—her parents were kind of hands-off—so I thought it made perfect sense for me to take a break from my parents and move in with her after the diary fiasco. My mother said no (of course she did, she was a rational parent), but at the time I was completely horrified that she wouldn't support the move in light of her betrayal.

Nothing else came of that kiss with Kyle. It was fun, and kind of gross, and we never hooked up again.

But that was okay, because Chad Burke came along soon after that.

On November 19, 1993, I told my parents I was headed to—surprise!—Stephanie's house. It was my senior year, and I was about a month into dating Chad. He was friends with some guys who were in a fraternity at UW, so we drove to the campus to crash one of their parties. We were in the frat house, deep into our red Solo cups of jungle juice, and suddenly Chad grabbed my hands, looked into my eyes, and said: "Anna, I want you to lose your virginity to me."

"Okay, Chad," I said solemnly. "Me too."

Chad couldn't say he wanted *us* to lose our virginity *together*, because it was going to be his second time. He slept with another girl in our high school before he and I got together (I can't remember her name, only that she looked like Ani DiFranco), but they were never in a relationship. I found his honesty about this romantic—my standards were always exceedingly high.

I told Chad I wanted to wait until after I turned seventeen.

I don't know why that age marker was important to me, but my birthday was ten days later, so I figured we wouldn't have to wait much longer. After that, I told him, I wanted to do it.

The plan didn't quite pan out. I turned seventeen on November 29, and a few days later, before Chad and I had the chance to have sex, I started hemorrhaging out of my vagina.

It started out as what my mom told me was my "first very heavy period." I had to change my pad every thirty minutes and it seemed more intense than a period, but what did I know? I was only seventeen. As an early Christmas present, Chad took me to see *Phantom of the Opera* and I had to keep running to the bathroom and begging people for tampons because I'd used up all of mine. Eventually I bled through my dress and Chad took me home. My mom told me to take a bath and we watched as the tub filled up with blood. Later that night we went to the hospital, and I passed out in the waiting room.

It turned out I was having some crazy hemorrhaging where I lost about 50 percent of my blood in three days. I had a cyst on my right ovary—the particularly gnarly kind that has hair and teeth and is just incredibly gross. So I ended up staying in the hospital for about a week, which is, oddly enough, an incredibly happy memory for me, because I really hated high school.

The doctor I saw during that ordeal became my gynecologist, and at some point I had the opportunity to tell her that I really wanted to have sex with my boyfriend and that (1) my mom couldn't know and (2) I could not get pregnant. So she put me on birth control, which she told my mother was to better regulate my cycle.

By January, I was a new, healthy woman—and a woman on birth control, no less.

Senior year we were allowed to leave school during lunchtime, and Chad's parents both worked, so on January 7 I told him I wanted to lose my virginity during lunch. So that's what we did. And it was horrible.

No, it wasn't really horrible. It was a solid C. I certainly didn't come, but nobody comes their first time. At that point in my life, I had never masturbated. I had never even explored, so I had no help to offer Chad in terms of getting me off. But I wasn't really in it for the sexual pleasure. I was just head over heels for this guy, and at the time I thought if I was going to keep a man I had to give him my pussy over lunchtime at his parents' house. In retrospect, his mother must have known. We were totally inconsiderate and never even thought about changing the sheets. Poor Mrs. Burke.

After we had sex, Chad and I went back to school and I felt the weird illogical pride of having lost my virginity. That afternoon I went to my neighbor Kate's house—she went to a rival high school and was incredibly hot and popular and was the head of the dance team and had a great laugh and stunning smile and was funny and charming and had lost her virginity long before me—and her mom looked at me and said, "Something looks different about you. You lost your virginity." I know that sounds like something Amy Poehler said in *Mean Girls* but she really did say that, and I loved the confirmation that I suddenly seemed more adult.

Of course, it took me many more years of sex before I felt any confidence or comfort when it came to doing it. If it hadn't been for my massive insecurity about my body, I probably would have been incredibly promiscuous. I was totally intoxicated with the idea of feeling like a sexual being, and I wanted men to want me. But I was also completely ashamed of my body, especially my boobs (or lack thereof), and insecure about my abilities as a lover. I never felt like the hot girl, even though I so badly wanted to. I felt like I wasn't good enough, and that I didn't know what I was doing when it came to sex or going down on a guy. And when I did get intimate, I was so busy thinking about my own performance that I couldn't appreciate the guy's, and it's really hard to have an orgasm when you can't let that part of your brain go.

I've grown out of that, thank God, but it took me a long time to get there. Today, I love being intimate with a partner, but I have a lot of trouble being intimate with myself. For a while in my late teens, on the other hand, I was just the opposite. Freshman year of college, I went through a crazy masturbation phase. We had this college newspaper with an advice column and one time a reader wrote in and said, "My roommate masturbates all the time, what am I supposed to do about it?" I read it and thought, *Oh man, she's talking about me.* To this day, I'm pretty sure I'm right about that, and that the letter was indeed about me. My roommate, Melissa, had a boyfriend who would call our room while she was at work and ask me about masturbating, so I'm convinced she said to him: "Oh God, I'm rooming with this gross girl, Anna, and she gets herself off all the time."

Melissa didn't like me very much. (Considering that last paragraph, maybe that's not a huge surprise.) We had one of those communal shower situations in our dorm bathroom, and one time she came in and started throwing her shampoo and conditioner at me because she was mad that I didn't wake her up for her exam. I was so confused (and still am!), because I didn't know that was my responsibility.

I ended up leaving that dorm—not because of my excessive masturbation but because Melissa and I clearly didn't get along—and I moved into a different dorm with a sweet roommate who at one point asked me why they call it a blow job.

"I don't know," I said. "Because you blow?"

That's totally incorrect, of course. It's actually because a guy blows his load in your mouth and not about us at all. Big surprise.

I got it out of my system, and I have an irrational fear that someone is watching me whenever I'm intimate with myself. I know that's ridiculous, but it's hard to shut off all the insanity that's going on in my brain at any given time. I feel like getting myself off would force me to confront the things that terrify me about myself, and to face sexual desires I don't even know I have. Masturbation acknowledges your sexuality in a way that we never did in my household, and while it was easy to get stoned in college and block out those childhood messages, as an adult I find it surprisingly difficult. Which perhaps is why I still feel an incredible amount of shame when it comes to self-pleasure. Once, when Chris was traveling for work, Allison Janney and I were talking on the set of *Mom*. "Chris is gone and I haven't masturbated in four months," I told her. "I don't know what's wrong with me. I think I probably should, but I can't."

Allison just looked at me and said, "Oh, honey, you've got to work on that."

Needless to say, I've got a complicated relationship with masturbation. I think we can all agree that men don't find themselves in that predicament.

F or a lot of women, the four years of college are a time of sexual experimentation and, in some ways, I definitely wanted that experience for myself. I loved going to frat parties and flirting with boys, but then I would get wasted and run away as fast as I could. I felt like the definition of a cocktease.

There were definitely a few times when it got a little scary, most notably during my sophomore year. I was talking with a guy at a party when I told him I had to pee. He said I could use one of the bathrooms upstairs. In fact, he had a private one in his room! How convenient! He said he'd show me the way and went into the bathroom with me, locked the door behind him and started trying to make out with me. "This is not fucking happening," I said. Maybe I didn't use those exact words, but close, so he left and locked the door from the outside. I was stuck in the bathroom and could hear him in the hallway talking to his friends, saying something like, "I got this; it's all good." I turned into that mother who can suddenly lift a car when her baby is trapped underneath—I heard this guy with his friends and just thought, *I am a warrior and I'm getting the fuck out of here.* So I picked the lock—which was not especially hard, it's not like I'm a champion lock picker— and I made my escape. These days, there's a lot of talk about college sexual assault, but that conversation was not happening in 1995, it was just "you get drunk at a frat house and it's up to you." So I channeled my inner ninja and dealt with it.

I have had one one-night stand in my life. After Chad Burke, I dated a guy named Dave on and off for most of my college career. During one of the off periods, I had a drunk night with some guys who lived on the floor above me in my dorm. We were all drinking and laughing about something stupid in their room, and I saw one of the guys look over to his roommate and give him a head jerk that clearly said, "Time to leave, wingman." You know when you're wasted but then something happens that jolts you back to reality? That head nod did the trick. The roommate understood the signal and left, and the other guy and I started kissing. Suddenly he was on top of me, and I said no, and he stopped, groaning, "Oh fuuuuuuck," mostly to himself, in a clearly frustrated tone. I didn't want to annoy him or be a tease, so I gave in. I was pretty resigned and unsure, but I said okay. I gave consent. Still, it's not a good memory. I was so disappointed in myself for conceding, and despite having spent plenty of time wishing I was more sexually daring, that wasn't a great night.

It wasn't all sexual nightmares, of course. There were good times, too, though the best of those came later. About a decade later, but they came.

# Listener Advice: I Was the Short Girl. What Were You?

I grew up in a tall family. My mom is five seven and my brother is six four and my dad's side is all very tall, too. I even have a female cousin who is six one. But I was always the little one. At home, in school, in theater, everywhere. This is perhaps most apparent in elementary school class photos, where I am always relegated to the end of the front row, about a foot shorter than everyone else. I was young for my grade— I started kindergarten when I was four—so that may have contributed, but the height discrepancy was more than just an age thing. By fourth grade, my parents considered sending me to a growth specialist, where I would be injected with hormones. They decided against it, and around junior year of high school I finally started growing. Today, I'm five four. Not tall, certainly, but fairly average.

Still, as a kid, being the short girl became my identity. It made me into a little Napoleon. I was insecure at school, and

SEAVIEW
HEIGHTS
ELEMENTARY
SCHOOL
GRADE 2-3
MRS. BEEM
1983-1984

I covered that up by being loud and bossy at home. It didn't help that I felt like I lived in the shadow of my older brother, Bob, who I couldn't stand. Today, I adore him. He's a professor of sociology at UC Davis who specializes in bullying and has worked with Anderson Cooper to raise awareness about what it's like to be a teenager in today's world. But back then, when the two of us were teenagers, we hated each other. He was a big tough guy, and I was a tiny short girl, and he generally overpowered me.

I had all of two victories over Bob when we were kids. The first was during a snow day. We rarely got snow days in Edmonds, because the city is close to the water, so it doesn't snow much. Always rain, never snow. One day when school actually did get canceled due to the weather, we were out in the driveway and he threw a snowball at me that landed smack in the middle of my face. So I reacted quickly and threw one right back at him . . . and nailed him right in the nose. I couldn't believe it! It was the first time I showed any hand–eye coordination in my life. The shock on his face was priceless. Of course, then he ran at me and grabbed me by the neck and shoved my face in the snow, but I was still euphoric. What a victory! The short girl had won!

My brother is three years older than I am. I spent a lot of my childhood running around the house yelling, "I hate Bob so much! I hate him, Mom!" And she would give me the classic "One day you guys will get along," and I hated her, too, for saying that.

I seriously couldn't imagine us ever being friends. But now we are. Incredibly. Maybe, sometimes, Mom does know best.

(There was one time—one time!—growing up when my brother was not the worst. I'll never forget it. I was in eighth grade and Kate, my neighbor, was one of my best friends. Most of my guy friends at the time were only friends with me because they wanted to get close to her. You'd think I would have resented that fact or, at the very least, that it would have offended my proud fourteen-year-old sensibilities, but mostly I loved it because it was attention, and, even better, attention from boys. One day Kate found out that some lame dude we knew said I was "homely" behind my back. I told Bob, and he called this guy and said something to the effect of "I'm going to fucking kick your fucking ass; I'm going to kill you." He scared the shit out of this guy, and Kate and I were listening in on the other phone—this was back in the days of landlines, when it was far easier to eavesdrop—and I couldn't believe my brother came to my rescue like that. He loved me! It was very sweet, but apart from that we didn't have much communication until I was older and we were both living in California. Now we're very close.)

Anyway, being the short girl totally infiltrated my psyche, not just because everyone in my life was tall, but because being small led me to feel like I wasn't respected or heard, and those feelings were a huge part of my life as a kid. They defined a lot about me in terms of how I related to friends and boys, and I think that sentiment was one of the main contributors to what I call my "proud and angry" phase, which I think was an attempt to overcompensate for my small stature.

Since all that, I've become a little bit obsessed with that one-word adjective that people use to describe you when you're young. You've had that experience, haven't you, dear reader? It's not just me, is it? I've always wanted to explore that question—can other people relate to that simple identifying adjective, or am I crazy? Have you been described as the rebel or the Asian or the goody-goody?

One of the biggest rewards of doing a podcast has been learning that all the weird shit we go through, other people have been there, too. More often than not, those defining experiences that can make us feel weird or lonely or embarrassed are actually universal. So I decided to poll my listeners, to hear their stories but also to find out if other people have let these childhood labels define them like I did, and to learn how they overcame it. What resulted was an overwhelming chorus of stories that reminded me that we're all in this together and that being a kid can be fucking hard.

Here's a sampling of the amazing responses, all of which gave me comfort in the knowledge that we've all been there.

---

Growing up, I never knew what to do in awkward or sad situations, so I'd just make a goofy face or tell a bad joke to ease the tension. Everyone would laugh and things would go back to normal, which made me happy. But whenever I was introduced to people, my friends would say, "This is Christina, she's the goofy one of the group." Being labeled "goofy" as you're growing up and trying to figure out who you are as a woman and how you relate to men was like climbing a mountain. I didn't want guys to see me as "goofy." I wanted them to see me as sexy or intelligent or able to lift heavy boxes. ANYTHING except "the goofy girl." For a long time, it made me believe that I didn't deserve love and I would be forever relegated to the best-friend role, the main character's sidekick who helped set up everyone except herself. As I got older, though, I realized that I want to enjoy life as much as possible with as much humor as I can. And that means I want to find someone who is just as goofy as me to laugh my way through life with. Now I shout off the rooftops, "I am goofy, and I'm damn proud of it!"

—Christina

———————————————

I was the weird cat girl. At my first boy-girl party, a gaggle of us went for a moonlit walk. One of the boys brought a BB gun and was going to shoot a cat with it. Just for fun. Horrified, I picked up the cat and refused to put it down until we got back to the house, where the gun would be put away. That night was the end of any hope I had for being popular ever again. That, and I accidentally wore a sweater to school (the same year) that my cat had peed on.

—Catherine

I was definitely the goody-goody growing up. Some of that was based on my actions, but most of it was that I was quiet and shy and studious, and people perceived that as being a Goody Two-shoes. Even now, at twenty-five, I have a hard time shaking that image. Anytime I do anything that doesn't fit that image, people claim it's *so* not like me, even though it's who I've been the whole time. I'm studying human sexuality, I have two tattoos, and I started occasionally doing live storytelling events; all of these choices have been met with shock and awe from the people who claim to know me best but who can't see past that label from my childhood.

—Tara

I was the only female redhead in my grade in elementary school, and to make matters worse, my hair was approximately five times the size of my head. So I was known as "the redhead" or "puffball" because of my puffy hair. As I got older, the names got worse. In first grade, kids said I couldn't sit with them because I had red hair. In sixth grade, a kindergartener told me my hair made me scary. By the time I got to high school, I was "ginger" and "fire crotch." People couldn't see past the hair. I begged my parents to let me dye it, but they wouldn't. I never had a real relationship in high school or college. People would tell me that I was too different to ever find love or that I was "pretty . . . for a redhead." Today, I'm extremely grateful my parents didn't let me change my hair color. I still tend to straighten it, out of the fear that it will look too thick and "puffy" if I don't. But, I like being different now.

—Jenny

---

I was always known as "the oldest." I'm older than my brother, so I always took care of him. To this day I feel the need to treat him like a baby, and we are in our thirties! I'm also the oldest grandchild, so that left me always having to babysit my cousins, always being the "responsible" one, always having to set the example. It's still hard for me to cry or show any type of vulnerability because I always have to be the strong one.

—Vanessa

I was the quiet one. I actually became increasingly shy as I grew up because that's what I was told I was. It was difficult to get over it, but now I'm able to talk to strangers and make eye contact without turning bright red. I was always quiet, but a lot of the time I was just observing what was going on around me. I'm still observant, but I no longer see it as a bad thing. I learn things about people, and I actually listen to what they have to say.

—Siobhan

"The best friend." As in, the person all the dudes confide in about wanting to date your friends, but never you. It has persisted through adult life and stopped only in the last few years (I'm twenty-eight). After a while it's hard not to see yourself as the one people confide in rather than the object of their affection. It's a ridiculous trope that

unfortunately was so true for me from ages thirteen
to twenty-five.

—Maddie

———————————

The lesson here? Screw the labels. But also, there's power
in sharing our stories.

Also, did I mention that you guys are awesome?

# Proud and Angry

In August 2016, Patti Stanger, the Millionaire Matchmaker herself, appeared on an episode of *Anna Faris Is Unqualified* and told a female caller that to attract a man at a bar, she should simply "smile and signal." No approaching a man, Patti said, not even to ask the time or the score of the game.

It was an eye-opening strategy for me, since for a long time my approach was pretty much the opposite of smile and signal. Instead, I called it "proud and angry."

For a long time, I had incredibly low expectations of men, and I felt so smug every time a guy proved me right. I loved manipulating them into doing something to show they were as shitty as I thought they were.

It started in college. In the nineties, the University of Washington had about forty Greek houses and for whatever reason (or, for a very specific reason named Chad Burke) I wanted to lash out at them. And so I would crash their frat parties.

It was my freshman year, but I looked quite young. As the

daughter of a sociologist (my dad was a professor before join-
ing the advertising world), the concept of field studies was a
familiar—and enticing—one. So I decided to conduct them at
the fraternities. I played this really fucked-up game where I
would crash their parties wearing tiny Catholic schoolgirl skirts
and raver boots with garter belts and stockings and little crop
tops. When I walked into the fraternities, I was clearly not a
sorority girl. There was this rhythm I found. Guys would talk
to me briefly and then say, "Do you want a tour of the house?"
which I learned meant, "Do you want to go to my bedroom?"
They barely talked to me before inviting me for the "tour." I
was in such an angry place that I loved the idea of guys validat-
ing what I already thought I knew—*Men don't want to get to
know anybody! They just want to take advantage of women!*—and
they almost always did. I wouldn't actually cash in on the bedroom invite, I just used it as proof that guys were as scummy as
I thought they were.

Then I started creating this charade where I would pretend to be a fourteen-year-old high school student whose sister, Meghan, was a Tri Delt. Meghan was at the party, I'd say,
but nowhere to be found. The test, as I saw it, was simple: "Is
this guy going to try to fuck a fourteen-year-old?" The answer was always yes. Though, I should clarify that I probably
didn't actually look fourteen. And I was probably sort-of
known because I went to school there and had hung out at
fraternities before. And I was playing a very flirtatious
fourteen-year-old. So in defense of the fraternity guys at UW
who aren't scum, which is probably most of them, I should

point out that perhaps they weren't all perfectly willing to screw a fourteen-year-old and commit statutory rape. It was not a very scientific experiment.

I'm not entirely sure why I was so proud and angry. I think part of it was just being a college kid who didn't realize that it was okay to admit ignorance about something. There was so much I didn't know and hadn't experienced, and instead of owning up to that, I thought behaving like a confident cynic would fool people into thinking I had everything figured out. But the facade also came from what I imagine was a very common goal of reinventing yourself when you get to college. Once I got to UW, I jumped at the chance to shed my theater nerd stature from high school. I did that by dressing unbelievably inappropriately. I'd wear the same plaid skirts and garter belts that I wore to the frat parties around campus. My brother, who was a senior when I was a freshman, once spotted me smoking a cigarette and dressed like I was going to a rave and marched over to me and said, "What the fuck are you doing?" He was appalled. That was when he was engaged to his first wife and about to graduate and was a brilliant academic. You know how in some families the siblings flip-flop who is the favorite and who is the black sheep? At that stage I was the bad kid and he was the star. (We traded roles for a while, but finally, at forty and forty-three, we're on equal footing. He's a professor who helps prevent the bullying of young kids; I cameo as coked-up versions of myself in films named for cats.)

My proud and angry bit inspired other weird practices that, looking back, are even more bizarre than I realized. For example, for a long time in college I loved doing this strange card trick that was basically an inside joke with myself. I would ask people to draw a card and I'd explain that I was actually a card reader and could tell them their destiny. No matter what card they drew I would say the same thing. "Oh, you drew the jack of diamonds," or nine of spades, or whatever. "That means you are really creative. You have some obstacles ahead of you, because you don't know how to achieve the leadership role you're destined for." Just the idea that I could say the same thing to every person and they'd always be like, "Oh my God, that's so true," made me feel superior. In retrospect, it's odd and disturbing that I took such pleasure in people living up to my low expectations of them, but it served as confirmation that my loneliness—because I didn't have a ton of close friends—was warranted. *This is why I'm lonely*, I'd think. *These people are minions.* When truthfully, other people's intelligence level had nothing to do with why I didn't have a close circle of friends. It was that I was shut off and relished my loneliness and I baited people to give me what I was looking for.

There was also this game I played when I studied abroad in Italy in which I would jumble up English words to "test" Italian men. So if I was talking to an Italian guy who was fluent in English, I would say "power feeling" instead of power trip, for example. The test was *Is this guy going to pretend to understand me?* It was weird, especially since I was basically just mocking someone's admirable attempt at speaking another language. I don't know where I got that from, or why I wanted people to let me down. I think there was an element of guarding myself against rejection—you are going to disappoint me, so I have to reject you first.

Maybe I played up the proud and angry persona because I was always attracted to those same qualities in men. I don't know why. I didn't date much, but there were maybe one or two nice guys I went on a couple of dates with who I remember not being interested in. It had nothing to do with their level of attractiveness—I just wanted an asshole.

I don't know why women are always attracted to bad guys. Even after being one of those women, I still don't get it. In my case, I was partially drawn to that kind of person because I was a late bloomer and I didn't feel very attractive, so any time someone remotely good-looking glanced my way, I fell hard for him—and I think asshole guys can sense that and take advantage of it. But I shouldn't tie that to gender. Guys fall all the time for women who are perhaps not the most stimulating other than their physicality, and it's the same thing. A person is willing to put up with a lot when they're just so grateful for the attention.

I don't know when the shift happens to realizing, *Oh yeah, I actually like being with someone who is interesting or makes me laugh or makes me feel good, or at least someone who doesn't belittle me or make me feel bad.* I certainly don't think all my exes intentionally wanted me to feel shitty, I just think that was part of the narcissistic type that I was really drawn to.

Basically, I spent way too long subscribing to the proud and angry approach—the trappings of a youthful immature person. I should have just smiled and signaled.

# Turning the Tables:
# Not-So-Rapid Fire

Since we started the *Unqualified* podcast, our guests have been good sports when it comes to the recurring segments, which can be silly and, sometimes, kind of wild. But we've never turned the tables. I've never been on the receiving end of "Not-So-Rapid Fire" or "How Would You Proceed?" or "Deal Breakers," so I decided to put myself in the hot seat for this book. I asked my friend Cassie Daniels, a screenwriter and a segment producer on the podcast, to put together some questions and surprise me with the classic *Unqualified* treatment—and it made me weirdly nervous. It's odd to be on the opposite end. I feel like I need to call all our guests and apologize.

## NOT-SO-RAPID FIRE
## WITH ANNA FARIS

*Would you rather lose your orgasm or your sense of humor?*

My orgasm. It would be sad, though. And the two are kind of linked, aren't they? If you're in a happy place and relaxed and really love your partner, it's so much easier to have an orgasm. And I can't be in a relaxed happy place with someone who doesn't make me laugh. But! If the two were completely separate then, yes, definitely the orgasm.

*What's your survival plan for a zombie apocalypse?*

I've actually been told that I should head immediately to the west side Ace Hardware because the whole building is surrounded by high, curved metal fences that the zombies can't get into, and we would have plenty of supplies like shovels. It was the Yuan twins, who worked on *Observe and Report* and have written a zombie film themselves, who told me that.

"Well, what can I bring?" I asked.

"We're not even quite sure we're going to let you in yet, actually," they said. "Because you aren't going to offer a lot."

"What if I offered comedic monologues to keep the morale high?"

"Well, you'd still be taking our water supply," they said.

So I offered to help procreate, but they were iffy on that, too, so I guess if they didn't let me in I'd stay at my house and I'd let people come over. I've got a nice candelabra and some weaponry to smash a zombie's brains in, and lots of earthquake survival kits that my mom gives me every Christmas.

*Think of this like "fuck, marry, kill" but instead you have to hide a dead body with someone, call them to bail you out of jail, or get anal bleaching together. And it's the costar edition. Here are your options: Allison Janney, Regina Hall, Emma Stone.*

I think I would hide the dead body with Regina, because she's pretty cool under fire. She wouldn't panic under the stress of that. I'd call Emma Stone to get out of jail, because she's really crafty and quick on her feet and she would create a plan. I think she would be a little surprised to hear from me, though, because it's been a while. "Hey, Emma! I'm in a little jam!" But I think she would answer the call. And then Allison, yeah, we could do anal bleaching. We've seen a lot of each other's bodies. But truly, I think any of these women would perform well in any of these scenarios.

*If you could erase one audition from your memory, what would it be?*

There was an audition I did in college—I can't even remember what play it was for anymore—but it was at the ACT Theatre in Seattle and I remember working really hard to prepare and knowing from the moment I opened my mouth that they weren't into me. I did a monologue and then I read from the script with another actor and I knew I was tanking. I wasn't doing well in my theater classes at the time, either. After the audition, I ran into an older actor outside the theater who told me that if I can do anything else, I should.

"Do you want to act?" he asked me.

I said I thought I did.

"Are you any good at anything else?" he asked.

I said that yeah, I probably was.

"Then that's what you should do," he said. "If it's not torment to not act, then you shouldn't act."

So I thought, *Okay, I'm not going to act anymore.* I dropped out of the drama program at UW and went into comparative literature, and then Greek mythology, and then communications, before I finally landed on an English major. That was the audition that made me say, "All signs are pointing to me not being an actor." I felt a little bit bummed about it, but the idea had been growing in me for a bit. I was practical and realistic and I had already worked with enough struggling actors to feel confident that I wasn't going to just go to Hollywood and make money acting.

So I stopped. But I had a Seattle-based agent already, so I thought, *If she calls me I'll still audition for commercial things in case I can make a little money here and there.* And she did call, about a horror film that would eventually pull me back to acting.

*If you had a wrestling move, what would it be called and what would it be? And what would your wrestling name be?*

The move would be the Faris Wheel Fairdown. It would involve me being in a handstand and swiveling my legs and wrapping my ankles around my opponent's neck and taking them out headfirst. It would be pretty dramatic. My wrestling name would be . . . the Ah-minator? Like, rhymes with Dominator? That doesn't make a ton of sense, but she'd be a pink dominatrix.

*You are serving seven years and four months at a maximum-security prison in Wichita. What are you in for and what is your prison job?*

Easy. I'm in for using a big Bowie knife to stab and murder a home invasion burglar who ended up being unarmed. I stabbed him, maybe, twenty-four times. So the big question became, Was this self-protection? Maybe it was an acquaintance or someone I knew a long time ago, so while it seemed like maybe he came to rob me, the details are a little hazy. But I thought he was trying to rob me when I stabbed him, or that was my defense at least.

I would like to say that I'd work in the prison library, but I think I'm too chatty, so I think I'd want to do food service. But not dishwashing, though I'd probably have to work my way up. Or I could do laundry, but there's a lot of noise there, so I wouldn't get to be too chatty. My volunteer work would be in the theater program. *The Glass Menagerie* over and over again. Sometimes I would play Laura and sometimes I'd be the gentleman caller.

This doesn't sound too bad, actually. Maybe I should stab someone twenty-four times to get to do this. I would excel in prison. I do like to make the best of a bad situation, and I don't like drama, so I'm not going to be starting shit. I would learn to lay low until I got theater respect.

*Who was the bigger gold digger: Belle or Aladdin?*

With Belle, I think the whole thing was about aesthetic, so I've got to go with Aladdin. But I am fascinated with successful real-life gold diggers. They're amazing to me. You see them a lot on *Real Housewives*, and it's an art. How do you get elevated to marriage status? It's a big red flag when a hot young girl has been with a rich guy for six or seven years and there still isn't commitment. A successful gold digger makes it happen in the first two years. The proposal isn't going to happen if you got too far down the road. Here's what I think it takes to get to marriage: The girl can't have slept with any of the man's friends. She has to give good blow jobs. She has to be mildly flirtatious with the guy's friends but not too much, because the friends always have the guy's ear. She has to be very pleasant and laugh at everyone's jokes. It sounds exhausting.

*Would you rather eat your own placenta or be in labor for seventy-two hours without an epidural?*

For sure eat my own placenta. I'm not thrilled about that idea, don't get me wrong, but when I was in labor before my epidural, that was like nothing I've ever known. I always thought, until that day, that I had a high pain tolerance. I still think I do—but labor is a whole other kind of pain. Next time, if I were to ever get pregnant again, I would know when to start asking for the drugs. You think the epidural is going to be some quick thing and that you have time before you need to ask for it, but no, it's a whole production—you need to sign consent forms and your husband has to leave the room. Contractions are a mind-numbing pain. I remember Chris complimented me, like, "Babe, you didn't even scream!" And I said, "Because I couldn't. I was so consumed. I had nothing in me." I remember in the moment telling myself, *There is going to be a time where I am going to forget this pain. Anna, do not forget. Do not forget do not forget do not forget.* But then you do.

# Waiting...

I was lucky to land a gig early enough into my time in LA that I didn't have to do the whole waiting tables while hoping for my big-break thing. But that doesn't mean I haven't done my time in food service.

In college, I waited tables at a high-end retirement home. Not because I love spending time with the elderly or because I felt like this would be more meaningful work than serving rich finance guys. I wish I was that good of a person. It was just that the other restaurants I applied to wanted me to be a hostess first, while at Ida Culver House Broadview, I could immediately be a waitress. I figured I could wait tables for a bit, then I could leave and get a better waitress position at a fancy restaurant soon after. I got $5.25 an hour, no tips. Not until Christmas, at least. The other workers there kept telling me to "just wait until Christmas." For what? Some old dude to give me fifteen bucks?

It was tough work. Not only is it grueling to be on your feet all day, but it's also so incredibly boring to listen to people tell you what they want to eat. Figuring out how to focus on the words coming out of people's mouths while they told me their food order was seriously my biggest challenge.

Of course, it didn't help that I would go to work stoned, and I'm not a good stoner. (Despite repeated references to smoking weed in this book, the activity actually makes me paranoid and weird and that's why I don't do it anymore.) Once I was taking the order of a four-top—four little German ladies in their late eighties who sat together every dinner. They placed their orders and I said "Uh-huh, uh-huh, uh-huh" as I wrote everything on my pad. (I always used a pad. I don't understand those servers at fancy restaurants who don't use a pad. I memorize lines for a living but I would never be able to keep orders straight.) After the last lady put in her request, I walked back to the kitchen and looked down at my pad. It was all just scribbles. I hadn't written down any actual words. I went back to the table in a sweat trying to figure out what I was going to say. If these ladies had had dementia I would have had some hope, but no luck. They were a sharp posse. So I said something about a cook dropping their order, but it was still embarrassing. Especially since there were only four options on the menu.

Later that same week I spilled hot coffee on one of those little German ladies.

Bottom line: I lasted four months and didn't even make it to Christmas. I was going to school and trying to get homework done, and my glamorous waitressing days did not feel like my destiny. Plus, between bus fare and getting my uniform cleaned, I ended up losing money overall.

When I told my mother I couldn't do the retirement home job anymore, she was so disappointed in me. "You are not a quitter!" she said. "I did not raise a quitter."

All I could say was, "Maybe you did."

But I needed a job. My parents generously paid for my college, but that was it. I didn't have an allowance. (Poor me!) I did manage to patch together a handful of acting jobs that would cover me for a month or so at a time. Training videos, radio commercials. I did a health insurance training video for nurses and doctors in which I played a young woman who was being told she has cancer. The director was so impassioned, so intent on me finding the arc of my story. It was, to this day, the most dramatic work I've ever done.

But waiting tables, in some ways, still goes down as the hardest. Certainly the most thankless. Which is probably why I generally avoid going to restaurants. I'd much prefer ordering delivery or—my latest obsession—ordering through Postmates. That way, no one has to struggle to focus while I spell out what I want in my taco salad.

# Unqualified Advice:
## Should You Move for the Guy?

**S**o many of the questions that come into the *Unqualified* podcast involve women asking for permission to be leaders in their own lives. They want to make a decision about their career that doesn't take a romantic partner into account, or they want to make a choice based on love that is independent of their career, or their friends and family. Should I stay with the guy my friends don't like? Should I take the job that would take me away from my boyfriend?

A lot of those questions touch specifically on moving for a man. I understand the dilemma here. Making the decision to uproot your life in order to be with a guy can feel counter to what we were taught as young girls—to be independent, to make a life for yourself and not rely on a man. But feminism is about being empowered to choose the life you want, and if being with the man you love is what will make you happy, then there's nothing wrong with that. So, like I said, I see the dilemma.

Also, I should point out, I have personal experience with this. I've been down this road. If I'm very honest with myself, my ex-husband was a huge influence on my decision to move to LA. After graduation, I got a plane ticket to London and a temporary job at an ad agency that my dad helped me find through a connection. I had previously worked as a receptionist in an office my father ran, and it was one of the best jobs of my life. I loved it—probably in large part because my dad was the boss—so I was all set to work in the mailroom of a British agency and move in with a dear friend who'd relocated to London a year earlier for art school. I was going to start a life across the pond, but then I went to an audition for a horror film, *Lovers Lane*, in order to make a little extra cash. I got the role of a cheerleader who gets gutted. The movie was filming in Seattle, so I was a local hire. There were four professional actors on the film, and Ben was one of them. He was hot and had an agent and lived in LA, and we flirted a lot. But the whole time, I was very aware that I was the day player and not the big star, which was made even more clear to me every day when I had to change into my cheerleading outfit in the bathroom.

This sounds arrogant, I know, but after a few days of filming I definitely felt like, *Man, if these four actors that are younger than I am can live in LA and have agents and acting careers and travel to Seattle and stay in hotels and have trailers on set, maybe I can, too.* Performing with them gave me a lot of confidence, because I could keep up. So yes, I certainly had an optimistic sense of, *If they can do it maybe I should give it a whirl.* But there's no question that I also felt dizzily enamored of the young hot actor who was giving me attention.

The shoot took about twenty-one days, and shortly after it was over, I decided to give LA a try. It was a combination of wondering about Ben (we didn't date during filming, but we did flirt and make out) and also worrying that if I didn't give Hollywood a year, I might regret it. I had nothing to lose, so I figured, *All right, if a year from now I'm miserable, I'll pick up and move to London.*

My story is different than some of our callers', I know, because I wasn't moving only for the guy. There was a career element, too. And I was lucky because my parents supported my decision. In fact, they were thrilled. When I first told them that I wasn't going to pursue acting after graduation they were bummed because they really wanted me to follow my dream. But I was trying to be practical—I didn't think acting was going to work for me. I didn't know if I was good enough. In the end, though, my parents really encouraged my decision to move to LA. So much so that my mom gave me miles to take a trip to Hollywood before moving, and I stayed with my cousin's friend while I met with the manager who is still my manager today.

All this to say, I did move to LA to be an actress, but there's no question that Ben was part of the equation. Had I not met him, I might be living in London right now. It would provide me so many opportunities to use my cockney accent—I'm still waiting for my big Oscar-baiting period role—but thank God things didn't go that way. So while it's probably crazy to move to a new city just because the hunky guy you've been crushing on for three weeks lives there, things sometimes do work out.

Which, now that I think about it, isn't helpful advice at all and is totally self-involved unless you, dear reader, are also wondering if you should move to LA to be near your slasher-movie crush.

If you have a stable career that you love in the city of your dreams and the only argument for moving is that a guy will be there, there's certainly a good case to be made for staying put. I'm just trying to say that I understand why someone would consider uprooting for love. I did it for far less than love. More like lust.

As you read my advice here, I understand that my story may seem more like a cautionary tale than words of encouragement, considering I subsequently married and then divorced this person. But thanks to LA I have my career and my son, so I'm doing okay.

The lesson from all this, I think, is that there's nothing wrong with moving to be near the one you love. If that person makes you happy, and you can have your own life in the city where you two can be together, I say go for it. And if it doesn't feel right and you're only considering moving because you think you "should," then don't.

And if you're trying to cast a modern-day Eliza Doolittle, call me.

# The Wedding Hoopla

I'm not really into weddings.

It's not that I don't believe in marriage, obviously. In fact, while I take issue with the whole wedding-planning rigamarole, I do get swept up in the emotion of the event when I'm a guest. But the dramatic production of getting engaged and the over-the-top ceremony with hundreds of people, it all strikes me as antithetical to the end goal, which is to celebrate the union of the bride and groom.

I've had two weddings—the first was in Tahiti and the second was in Bali. (In both cases, my parents ended up semi-forcing us to do a later celebration in Washington for our family and friends, both of which turned into the weddings I was trying to avoid.) I realize as I write this that I sound like a stereotypical celebrity—"Oh, I'm soooooooo uninterested in weddings, so I just ran off and got married at a little resort in Bali where we did a soul-cleansing ritual before we offered our firstborn to that little old man from *Eat Pray Love*"—but I do think there's a good, or at least understandable, reason why so many people in the public eye have extremely small weddings. As an actress, you get more days than most people in which it feels like you are celebrating yourself. Whether it's a premiere or a photo shoot or a talk show appearance, all those feel like, *Okay, this day is all about me.* And sometimes it's awesome and sometimes it's not. Sometimes you want privacy, or for someone to not appear in your personal space every time a hair falls out of place. I know how lucky I am to have all that, and I certainly don't begrudge the people whose job it is to make sure that my hair is as it should be when we're taping an episode of *Mom*, but *not* having all that can feel special, too.

Now that I think about it, maybe my aversion to a big to-do has nothing to do with fame, because I've never been a wedding person. Kate, my neighbor friend, had a wedding book in third grade. It had the dress and the flowers and the whole shebang, but I had no interest. Wedding talk didn't make me angry or anything, I just didn't care about it. I've never been great with party planning or interested in making a fuss about giant celebrations and making everything look perfect, which is probably related to why my house looks as insane as it does, with an outdated kitchen and living room walls covered in stuffed elk heads. So nothing about the hoopla of weddings appealed to me.

It's not just the fuss. The modern rituals of weddings—the big surprise proposal, the bridal party, the show of it all— they make me uncomfortable.

I know. I'm a buzzkill. But a lot of women question those

outdated rituals, right? How can you not? Both Ben and Chris asked my father if it was okay to propose to me, and in both cases my dad said that while of course he thought it was very considerate of them to ask, it was "unnecessary because it is completely my daughter's choice." I thought that was pretty cool of him.

Who came up with the idea that an engagement should be some elaborate high-pressure surprise where you are essentially trapping a person? I don't know where along the way we became a culture that mandates "you must conceive of some crazy trickery that will later be deemed romantic." It's fun for the surpriser, but not the surprisee. And then there's some poor woman who's like, "Holy shit, should I be doing this? Well, I can't say no now that he's created a scavenger hunt leading me to a ring on a chain around my dog's neck, who then barked three times and my whole family—in from out of town!—jumped out from behind the couch to start the celebrations before I've even answered so . . . Okay! Yes! I do!"

The first time Ben proposed to me we were on our way to lunch with our friend Alex. We walked into an antique-watch store that also had a lot of jewelry. Ben looked at the wedding rings and said, "Which one do you like?"

"I don't know," I said. "I'm hungry. I want to go eat Mexican food."

"Just look," he said.

So I pointed to a vintage ring with a Victorian look and said, "I don't know, this one is kind of cool."

"I'd like to purchase this," Ben told the jeweler of the ring before getting down on one knee.

I think my exact words were: "No no no no no, this is not how this is happening." Alex was there, and we were on our way to eat burritos. I didn't even know if I wanted to marry Ben at all, but I certainly didn't want to commit in that moment with Alex and the jeweler watching. So he didn't buy the ring, and we left and ate burritos during a palpably tense meal.

Six or seven months later, Ben and I had a dinner reservation at the restaurant at the Mondrian Hotel and, over drinks, he said, "Why don't we stay the night?" It turned out he had booked a room and covered the bed in rose petals and when we got upstairs he got down on one knee and said all the nice things you might imagine for a marriage proposal. That's when I said yes.

I remember thinking in that moment that I didn't want to tell my parents. In retrospect, I should have examined that more.

The evening was supposed to be romantic, and I'm sure for most women it would have been. But I can't be alone in thinking there is an element of blindsiding to these moments. God forbid you're proposed to in a stadium on the jumbotron, at which point you will be the most hated person in the arena—and eventually the world, when the clip goes viral—if you say, "I don't know."

Once you accept a marriage proposal, the engagement takes over your life. It's all you talk about with your friends and your fiancé and your parents—and that's not me being negative, that's just fact. Then there's the whole bridesmaid thing of ranking your friends, which we've gotten into already but I'll repeat, it's weird. Plus the frantic energy of that moment three hours before the ceremony when the makeup artist can't be found and there's a crazy hubbub as everyone scrambles to find a replacement. Some people just get off on the drama.

All of that is why I always say a honeymoon is essential. There's a December twenty-sixth feeling to the day after your wedding, so you've got to have something to look forward to when you wake up that morning. The celebration that required all your attention for the last year is over, and that can be a letdown, even when you've griped your way through the whole thing.

I sound like such a grump. I do love everything that a wedding stands for. I have an entire podcast about relationships! I just think the wedding buildup is an especially trying time. It's a scenario in which people show their cards. Sometimes they step up to the plate in ways you wouldn't expect, and sometimes they let you down in ways you didn't anticipate.

An admission: when it comes to getting wrapped up in the wedding hoopla, I'm not totally innocent. I've had my moments.

Before I had two of my own—four, if you count the big celebrations I had at my parents' insistence—the first wedding I remember being a part of was my brother's wedding to his first wife. Their wedding was a big to-do and, probably out of obligation, the bride asked me to be in the bridal party. You know how that goes—I was at the end of the line of brides-maids, the new sister-in-law who the bride didn't know that well and probably didn't really like. We wore these plain, al-most Amish-looking pale pink dresses, which were incredibly unsexy. But that was fine, I didn't really care about how I looked—no one was looking at me—and I remember dancing a ton and having a great time and my brother being furious at me because I'd been late to the ceremony. But being a little late for the wedding was nothing, because I'd already cemented my place in the story of their nuptials at the rehearsal dinner.

I was twenty, and I was drunk. And so, the night before the wedding, I stood up and announced that I was ready to give the bride and groom a present: a monologue from the Carson McCullers play *The Member of the Wedding*. I can't believe my parents let me do this. I shudder to think of it—the little sister who thinks she's an actress delivering a dramatic reading from the point of view of a twelve-year-old girl who wants to be a part of her brother's wedding but also doesn't want to lose him. *How pretentious is that?!* I performed that monologue in front of nearly one hundred people and I can only imagine what my ex-sister-in-law must have been thinking. I literally prefaced it with "Ding ding ding, I want to give you both a gift!"

My brother and I have never spoken about this moment. I can't imagine he has anything complimentary to say about it, though he's been kind enough to avoid mocking me and he didn't even get back at me, despite the two weddings at which he could have.

Shortly before getting engaged, Ben and I traveled to

Tahiti, where we took an amazing island tour led by a local named Mako. When we were planning our wedding, I suggested inviting just our closest friends and family, having Mako take us all to the Tahitian islands, and doing a swimsuit wedding. Ben was cool with it. My parents, not as much.

"What do you mean?" my mom asked. "You're having a fourteen-person wedding in Tahiti? And that's *it*?"

"Yes," I said.

"So, what, it's just going to be us and your friends?"

"Yes."

"So I can't invite any of my friends?"

"Not really," I said.

"Well, fine, we'll come," she said. (I was paying for everything.) "But we're going to have a big party for you afterward."

It wouldn't have been practical to invite a huge crowd to Tahiti. There was a lot of getting in and out of boats, which was not an activity for a grandmother. I knew this was not the event my parents had imagined for their daughter, but in the end the wedding was just what I wanted. We spent the morning feeding stingrays and drinking beer on a boat with Mako and his ukulele-playing nephew. Then we went to the island where Mako's family lived. They made us fresh tuna with coconut milk and it was a collection of the people I treasured most, all salty and in our swimsuits and lightly buzzed. The night before the wedding, I came up with an idea I'm still proud of, and split the guests into two groups—one was tasked with coming up with an original dance, the other an original song. They blew it out of the water. It was an amazing wedding from start to finish and at the end of the night I was grinning from ear to ear, wearing my flower crown, and looking around at everyone's slightly burned cheeks. I felt like I had escaped the wedding mayhem I wanted nothing to do with. But then I spent the next two and a half years in a marriage that wasn't right for me. So there you go.

In an effort to smooth over the whole fourteen-person Tahitian affair with my parents, who had spent more than twenty-five years thinking they'd throw their daughter a big wedding, I agreed to let my mom host a party in Washington. It became a source of contention pretty quickly—I had 10 friends there and my parents had 180 and my mom bristled at any friends I suggested adding. But my parents were generous and footed the bill. It ended up being an especially crazy night for me because our families were completely dramatic about everything and my friends all did ecstasy and it was a little bit miserable, I hate to say. So that sort of reaffirmed my aversion to big weddings. I just don't understand going to all this trouble and spending all this money to have a big celebration and then being miserable and stressed throughout the whole thing.

**A**ll that said, when I'm at a wedding, I'm a sucker for the sentimentality. I don't cry very much in my own life, which is something I get from my mom. It's kind of a problem. I wish I cried more; it would probably be a good release for me, though not crying helps me deal with rejection—a good skill to have in my line of work. The only time I do find myself crying is at weddings, and despite my personal stance on bridal parties, I've actually been a bridesmaid seven times. I don't particularly like doing it, but I'm good at it. Granted, I'm bad with planning or organizing, but I'm great at being attentive to someone else and not really caring about what I look like, almost to a fault. I'm the first to acknowledge that this event is not about me. So while I do, admittedly, have a skeptical view of the wedding process, I recognize that there is something poignant and momentous to proclaiming your love for someone in front of a lot people, most of whom you love, or maybe at least like.

Chris and I did that, though not at first. In 2009, we traveled to a friend's wedding in Bali and we stayed on the island for a few days afterward for an extended vacation. We'd been together for two years, he'd already asked me to marry him, and we were staying at this incredible resort where we discovered there was an actual "wedding option" when you booked your room. So we decided to elope and got married that weekend, after all the guests left our friend's wedding. It was a gorgeous ceremony that was just the two of us. We had already told our parents that we were probably going to elope, and we'd promised them that we would have a party at home, too. It took us three years to make it happen, and we had a big celebration that ended up being the wedding we'd been trying to avoid, but this time it was pretty incredible. We hosted seventy people at a lodge in Washington. My dad officiated the ceremony, and it was exactly the way we wanted it.

There was some minor drama at the party, but I remember giggling my way through it because it reminded me of the beauty of elopement, which was just me and Chris. Nothing major happened at the party—just my cousins getting in a fistfight on the dance floor, and some of Chris's friends bringing strippers as dates, and then a girlfriend of one of Chris's friends accusing me of hitting on her boyfriend. On my wedding day.

Your average wedding hoopla. Who wouldn't want that?

# Unqualified Advice:
# Not Enough Soul

If there's one thing that the pursuit of romance and the pursuit of an acting career have in common, it's rejection. It's inevitable that the way you handle rejection in one of those arenas will inform how you face it in the other. For me, it feels a little like the chicken or the egg—the romantic rejection I've experienced has undoubtedly affected how I approach auditions, and the professional rejections I've received from casting agents has influenced how I approach relationships. And I've been acting for so long, and crushing on boys for so long, that I don't know which came first.

Let's start by recounting some of my most memorable professional rejections. There was the time I auditioned to play Joey's sister on *Friends*. It was Season 8, and there were maybe fifteen actresses in the waiting room, all recognizable people, and at the very end of my audition, one of the producers laughed audibly—a big *HA!*—and I thought, *Okay, I nailed this*. After I was done, some of the actresses were asked to stay, but I wasn't one of them. To the rest of us, the casting director just said thanks and sent us on our way. Everyone could see who was staying and who was going. As I walked out, filing past the row of women who still had a shot, the casting director poked her head out and said, "Anna? Why don't you stay?"

"Okay, great," I said, and headed back to my seat.

Then, thirty seconds later, there was her head again, peeking out the door. "Anna? You know what, it's fine. You can go."

I had to walk out—again—past all the other actresses. It was embarrassing, for sure, but there are benefits to being forced to face those moments. Namely, you build up the resilience it takes to pursue a career in Hollywood. Those moments mess with your head and pit actors against each other, but they have made me stronger, too.

Of course, that rejection made it all the sweeter when I was cast to play the birth mother of Chandler and Monica's babies in the final season. I was in a Best Buy when my agent called and said I got an offer to be in five episodes. Like everyone, I was a huge fan of the show and I was thrilled but terrified walking onto that set. There was a moment that I was alone onstage, and I got to sit on the couch at Central Perk and see the picture frame that surrounded the apartment peephole, and it was magical and surreal. It was *Friends* (!!) and it was the last season, and it was not lost on me what a big deal that was. (I basically had IBS the whole time.) As we taped, I could feel the cast growing more and more sentimental, and I was in this unusual position of being a complete stranger but also, because my minor role was important to the characters' stories, a part of their ending journey. During one run-through, Jennifer Aniston suggested a group hug and I was standing nearby so I started to take a step forward, but then I took a step back, I just didn't know where to go. It was like, *Should I? Do I belong here?* And then Matthew Perry gestured for me to come in, so I awkwardly joined the embrace, which was incredibly bizarre. But the cast was so welcoming, especially Matthew and Courteney Cox. They were both impressively emotionally invested in the Monica/Chandler/baby story line, which reinforced the idea for me that these were characters they'd fallen in love with over time. I felt the weight of that.

Long before I auditioned for *Friends*, I faced an even more noteworthy rejection after attempting to land a different TV role. I was auditioning for a network pilot—a beautiful drama that I was really eager to be a part of. I went to four auditions and I knew that I was in the final rounds to play the big and emotionally powerful role of the pregnant neighbor who moves in with the main character and her son. It was pilot season in the early 2000s. I was still very much finding my way in LA. I had done *Scary Movie* and taped a pilot about a talking dog, but those were the entirety of my Hollywood credits, so landing this kind of meaty role felt like a big deal. I was getting close, and it was down to me and two other girls, but my agent called me the day after the audition to tell me I didn't get the role. Then he started to laugh. "Your feedback was that you don't have enough soul," he said.

Not enough soul? What the fuck do I do with that? How do I get more soul?!

Usually, when you don't get a part, your agent will deliver the news but protect you from the really harsh criticism. They don't often reveal the notes, especially when a casting director says you're lacking talent or you aren't hot enough. In this case, I think my agent shared the feedback because it was so ridiculous. He didn't say it as if to imply I needed to actually get more soul, he was saying, "You're not going to believe this." He was coming from a place of believing in me, and he acted as if this was the most ridiculous feedback he'd ever heard. But all I could think was, *How do I interpret this rejection? How can I develop a soul that people will respond to?*

Professional rejection made me incredibly guarded when it comes to relationship rejection. The question of how to value myself if casting directors don't value me is a really hard one, and it's one I bet plenty of other actresses struggle with, too. I never wanted to reveal my hand in a romantic relationship until I knew the guy was digging me. I don't know if that's a wise move or if it's totally fucked-up. It definitely has a bit of an "I'll show you mine if you show me yours" edge to it. But when you constantly put yourself out there professionally, it's hard to do so emotionally, too.

And, similarly, when you are rejected romantically, whether it's the end of a long relationship or after just a single date, you question yourself there, too. If a person acknowledges they don't want to get to know you better or spend more time with you, you feel pretty shitty. The ego bruise can be profound, so how do you get over it?

After Chad Burke broke up with me at the beginning of college, I spent a long time wondering what I did wrong.

*Why does he want to move on from me?* I'd wonder, legitimately baffled. *My parents like me, why doesn't he?*

It wasn't until Dave, the on-again, off-again college boy-friend, came along, that I was able to move on. Accepting defeat has always been an issue for me, and I think that speaks to my determination (if we're being generous) or my pride (if we're being honest)—it's a fine line. In the past, when resisting defeat meant living in a state of disillusionment and trying to make a bad thing work, I did it. With men, I have stayed in relationships long past the time I should have bailed, but I never let the failure of one relationship deter me from the next. With acting, I emotionally invested myself into what might seem like the silliest of projects (see: frozen yogurt commercial; a Red Robin training video) and continued to audition, even when I didn't have enough soul.

Dave's arrival didn't suddenly erase the memory of Chad, or the sting of that rejection, of course. And meeting Ben didn't erase Dave, and Chris didn't erase Ben. But I take comfort in the idea that once you accept that certain relationships will always haunt you, they actually make you a better person. Because now you've experienced the pain of loss and heartbreak and, at least in my case, humiliation. I like to think that those breakups made me a more compassionate and empathetic person and, in turn, a better actress.

These days, I have a wonderful family and a steady job and I'm lucky not to have to deal with too much rejection on any given day. But I still find myself thinking about it a lot. Mostly when I watch *The Bachelor.* I love *The Bachelor* so much, and I can't help but feel for those contestants. They're thrown into a competitive frenzy where the fear of rejection probably forces them to feel an emotional attachment to a guy they don't know and probably don't even like that much. Can you imagine being on a date where you are legitimately, not just in theory, competing in the moment with other women? That must be so much harder than getting rejected from a one-on-one date. Of course they're crying! It's 4:00 A.M. and they're drunk and hungry and wondering why they didn't make the cut. I totally get that feeling. It's not about love for this stranger, but the knowledge that *I'm being compared to twenty other attractive women and I guess there's nothing about me that stands out.*

In other words, they probably didn't have enough soul.

# Meet My Parents

For much of my childhood, my mom chopped my hair into a distinctly dude-like bowl cut. I know this wasn't her intention, but it was a hairstyle that more or less guaranteed I wouldn't be flooded with compliments, which was ultimately a good thing. At least it nipped in the bud what my mom would say when I *was* told I looked cute in a dress or got complimented on my appearance in any way. "And she's also smart!" she'd always quickly add.

My parents were incredibly supportive and proud of me when I was growing up, and they still are. I'm unbelievably lucky. Reporters often ask me how my parents reacted when I told them I wanted to pursue acting, I guess because most actors' families are understandingly skeptical of the entertainment industry. But my parents were always enthusiastic—if not a little delusional—about my show business dreams, and I'm so grateful for that. They wanted me to follow my passion even at a young age, but they also worked hard to ensure I kept a good head on my shoulders despite whatever success came my way.

When I was eleven, I played Scout in a Seattle theater performance of *To Kill a Mockingbird*. It was a long run—four months, six shows a week—which was a lot for a little kid, and it was my first really big part. That's when acting became my identity and school sort of became a secondary focus. In advance of the opening, I was asked to appear on a morning radio show with the other cast members. So at 4:00 A.M., my parents drove me downtown and listened in on the interview, in which I talked about my starring role. I was in sixth grade, and I was stupid, and I put on a weird pretentious act for my first big radio appearance. I spoke as if *of course* I was the lead, and I tried to come off as self-aware and sophisticated while I talked about "the industry" and "my passion" in the way I thought an actor was supposed to. When the interview was over, my parents were so ashamed. They wouldn't talk to me for a full fifteen minutes—they were embarrassed, and didn't quite know what to say to me as a result, but it was harsh and I felt horrible. It was my first taste of press, so their disapproval stung especially hard. But they were right. I was being an eleven-year-old asshole.

I do think they loved that Scout performance, though. My parents still have this idea that I am destined for drama. After *Scary Movie 2* and *The Hot Chick* came out, my mom constantly commented that I was getting overlooked. "Oh, Anna, they just don't know what you can do," she'd say. "I want you to be Joan of Arc or Amelia Earhart." I could feel her frustration that Hollywood didn't understand her daughter. I know she thinks I could win Oscar after Oscar after Oscar if I was just given the chance, which is so incredibly loyal. Can you ask for anything more than that in a parent? I love that my mother will always have that hang-up. "You are so untapped, Anna," she says.

It's not like I've never done a serious film. I had small parts in *Lost in Translation* and *Brokeback Mountain*, both Oscar nominees for Best Picture, though my role in each was to add some levity to otherwise fairly somber movies. A producer of *Lost in Translation* and a dear family friend of the Coppolas had seen *Scary Movie,* so one day in May 2002, I got a call from my agent about an audition. It was a very hush-hush project—they didn't send me the script, and my agent didn't even know what he was sending me in for. But he told me they wanted me to audition that day, and I was still in the stage of my career where you drop everything if you get an audition, so I went to this obscure office building up on Mulholland. There weren't any other girls there. Normally if you go to an audition there are a handful of actresses waiting, but this was just me. So I walked into the office and it was me and Sofia Coppola. She was incredibly subdued, sitting with her video camera, and I started the scene. I hadn't been given any notes for the role, but from what I could gather, the character, Kelly, was an obnoxious actress, and I felt like I knew her. It was one of those moments where a role is so well written that I knew exactly what to do. So I got to the part where I start singing the karaoke song "Nobody Does It Better" by Carly Simon, and Sofia was laughing in her very subdued way, and I thought it was going well, and then we both heard the door handle start to jiggle. Sofia had locked it when we started, so we both stopped and stared at the handle, and finally she unlocked it and in walked Warren Beatty. It was just the three of us, and I immediately sat down and thought, *I guess this audition is over, because here's Warren Beatty.* They hugged, and Warren asked Sofia how her parents were doing.

"Good, they're in Thailand," Sofia said. "How's Annette?"

"Good, she and the boys are fishing up in Canada," Warren said. Then Sofia gestured to me and said, "This is Anna,

she was in . . . what were you in again?" So I told her about
*Scary Movie* and Warren turned and sort of registered me for
the first time and said, "Oh yeah, you were pretty fucking
funny."

The whole thing was like an out-of-body experience. I
had no idea what to do. Should I immediately excuse myself?
Should I talk to Warren Beatty? I felt like I was privy to all
these Hollywood secrets I shouldn't have been. The Coppolas
are in Thailand! Annette Bening's fishing in Canada!

When it was over, I walked back to my car feeling confident. But that was it. A couple of months went by, I didn't
hear anything, and I learned that a few of my friends had auditioned for the same role. I heard there was an offer out to a
big-name actress (I don't know who) and she refused it, so in
late September I was offered the role. It was funny, because I'd
always felt like it was mine, even when I heard they were
waiting on somebody else.

I showed up in Tokyo for the last week of shooting, so
everyone else had already been working together for a month.
I had a scene with Scarlett Johansson and Giovanni Ribisi and
their performances were so tonally muted, and then I came in
with my loud splashy character—some of the crew actually
had to adjust their mics—and I thought, *I'm really messing this
up. I don't get the tone of this film at all. Everything is wrong about
what I'm doing, but I don't know any other way.* It's tricky to come
into a movie at the end of filming. But I got over the fear and
ended up having an incredible time playing Kelly, and Sofia let
me do all kinds of ridiculous improv. In the best of ways, it felt

like a very unstructured environment, which, oddly enough, was the complete opposite of the weird rigidity of making a spoof movie, where every prop has to be in a specific place. *Lost in Translation* felt very fluid. You could walk in and out of the frame as you wanted and say what you wanted and Sofia would watch us and give notes in her quiet voice. It was very different from anything I'd experienced.

That role and *Brokeback* not withstanding, I'm usually tapped only for comedy. So after I took the movie *Smiley Face*, I sat my mother down to break the news. "Mom, I'm doing this movie and I'm so excited about it," I told her, knowing that I was wading into dangerous territory. "It's a weird indie about a girl who's stoned the whole movie and just wants weed."

"Oh, Annie," she said. (My mom calls me Annie, rhymes with *Connie*.) "You can't do that movie. You are a role model!"

She was so disappointed, but I had to explain to her—I *wasn't* a role model. I was known for a movie in which I got sprayed to the ceiling with cum. Today, it's normal for movies to be offensive, or at least to toe that line, but at the time it came out, *Scary Movie* was known for its raunch. It was one of the most offensive movies around, and it helped launch a genre of gross, distinctly un-role-modelish films.

"Mom, I love you so much and how supportive you are, and I could never pursue this career without you," I explained. "But as I'm going up for different roles or choosing projects, I really can't have your voice in the back of my head influencing my decisions." I wanted to play interesting characters and great people and horrible people and I couldn't reject opportunities that I really wanted to take on because I was worried about my mom, and she understood that.

When *Smiley Face* came out, my parents came to Sundance for the midnight screening and it was one of the best nights of my life. They laughed so hard. In fact, my dad was in such heavy hysterics I actually thought he might be having a heart attack, and it was so gratifying to see my mom doubled over in laughter, too.

Obviously having close, wonderful, supportive parents is a blessing. But a word of caution for any of you readers who are as lucky as I am in that department: You know those moments when your parents are so proud of you that they start bragging

about you in ways that are just horribly embarrassing? And even though, deep down, you love that they're shouting your praises to anyone who will listen, you are mostly just horrified? You know how you assumed that might end after high school? And then after college? And then, maybe after your first job? I'm here to tell you that, nope, it never ends. Especially from dad.

## EMBARRASSING, BUT ADORABLE, BUT MOSTLY EMBARRASSING DAD MOMENT #1

In 2007, I was tied to a biopic about porn star Linda Lovelace that I didn't end up appearing in. But when outlets first started reporting that I would be involved, *New York* magazine mentioned it with the headline ANNA FARIS SUCKS and added the slightly snarky line, "Her parents must be thrilled!" So my dad wrote an impassioned letter to the editor about their complicity in sexism in Hollywood and how they would never say that about a man, and they published it. "I am Anna's father," he wrote in a 264-word note that you can still read online. "It's an interesting question why actresses are criticized for the moral behavior of the characters they portray, but male actors are not. No one suggested that Robert De Niro's parents would be aghast at seeing him, as Al Capone, bash someone's head with a baseball bat. No one surmised that Al Pacino's mom would be mortified to see her son play a Michael Corleone who organizes uncounted brutal murders. No one raised an eyebrow at John Malkovich's decision to portray a would-be presidential assassin. And rightly so." He went on to explain that when a "talented, and brave, young actress" (thanks, Dad!) considers taking a controversial role, the media treats it differently.

It was so wonderful of my father but also mortifying.

## EMBARRASSING, BUT ADORABLE,
## BUT MOSTLY EMBARRASSING DAD MOMENT #2

My dad and one of our *Mom* writer-producers have developed a friendship based on music. My dad's a music aficionado and has thousands of CDs and vinyl records that clutter up the whole house and make my mom insane. Somehow my dad and this guy started bonding over old tracks and now they send each other their favorite recordings of, like, Bob Dylan at some obscure club in 1990. So one day I came to work and this colleague greeted me and said, laughing, "I have to tell you that your dad emailed me and said you were the best actress of your generation." *What?! Daaaaaad!* This guy very obviously didn't say that my dad was right. He was just like, "I thought it was really, really funny."

Again. Mortifying.

## EMBARRASSING, BUT ~~INFURIATING~~ ADORABLE, BUT
## MOSTLY EMBARRASSING DAD MOMENT #3

In middle school I was named a bus patrol crossing guard. It was a coveted gig that you had to be hand-selected for by the teachers. I led everyone to the bus in an orderly fashion and I had a pink slip so I could write people up if they misbehaved and I would do demonstrations once a year about what to do in case of an emergency, soberly explaining how you were supposed to exit the bus through the back door. It gave me such a high. I was so proud that I had made the cut and that I got to wear the special bus patrol vest, and I was especially stoked that I'd earned the gig on my own merit. Mr. Kincaid, the librarian who ran the program, could obviously see that I was a natural leader and therefore deserved the vest and the badge. Even though I was short and quiet, he could see I was worthy.

Years later, over dinner one night, my father revealed that he had called Mr. Kincaid when the big bus patrol crossing guard decision was being made. "Anna wants this more than she wants a pony," he'd said. "She may be short but please don't overlook her for bus patrol."

I was devastated. Even all those years later it messed with my head. Turns out I was chosen because my dad intervened and not at all because someone could finally see the little tyrant in me.

Really, really mortifying.

**M**y parents appeared on my podcast once. They were staying with me and I wanted to give our listeners a glimpse into who they are as a couple. They have a really impressive story in that they've been married since they were twenty-one and they have things figured out that not all of us do, like how to keep each other laughing after four decades.

And my brother and I are both really close with them, so that feels slightly unusual. (Or is it just unusual in Hollywood, which sometimes seems full of divorce and estranged family relationships?)

Despite their one fourteen-minute interview on *Anna Faris Is Unqualified*, my parents don't listen to the podcast. I sort of told them not to, and they sort of don't know how to, and I'm sort of grateful that they don't. As I'm recording, I certainly don't want to be thinking about how they'd react as I, I don't know, fake an orgasm. I expose myself in a totally different way during the podcast than I do when I'm acting because I'm not reciting somebody else's lines. It's all me, and we talk about stuff I would never ever dream of talking to my mom about, stuff she would scold me for talking about in front of her. Like vagina hair and blow jobs.

My parents have given me so much: the freedom and encouragement to pursue my dream, the model of a marriage to strive toward, and support through some really hard times. They also influenced some of the qualities that perhaps aren't always my best. My mom raised me to have a high level of emotional defense that has been very helpful for me as an actor but has also turned out to be a major character flaw. It's why I enjoy giving other people advice so much, rather than getting it for myself. Doling out guidance helps me to not get caught up in my own self-analysis. I think this stems from the Waspy idea of not talking about your feelings. It's also the reason my parents hate therapy, because they think it means admitting there's something really wrong with you. You should maintain a constant attempt at normalcy at all times, they would say. We're the kind of family where no one is allowed to be a victim, which is an overall good thing but makes it hard to admit to moments of sadness or hurt. Especially when you're reading about people stuck in refugee camps and you have good fortune and are in Hollywood and you're an actress making money who can splurge on, I don't know, a Chanel bag. I'm very aware of my good fortune.

That high emotional defense has defined who I am, but there's a lack of openness in that attitude. At this stage in my life I'm attempting to become more open (hence this book) and to tell my friends what's going on with me and to ask for advice, but I find it difficult. It just feels incredibly indulgent to talk about my "problems," which, in the scheme of things, aren't anything. I've been unusually fortunate. I was raised in a safe, happy home with loving parents, I have a healthy son, a supportive family and a great career, and whatever hitches there were along the way, most other people have had to overcome bigger shit, so how can I ask for sympathy? Not that my parents were constantly telling me to shut up and stop whining or anything like that—but it was a message I absorbed nonetheless.

I'm trying not to pass my high defense onto my son. There is so much that my parents did, and still do, for me that I want to do for Jack. I want to always provide him the best education I can, and encourage him to find a passion and pursue it, and to read him stories before bed at night, at least for as long as he'll let me. But, without sounding too much like a touchy-feely Hollywood mom, I'm proud when Jack can express his feelings in a healthy way. Recently, the two of us were home alone and Chris was out of town. Jack was acting a little withdrawn and was playing by himself quietly, which I haven't seen him to do very much. So I asked him, "Jack, is something bothering you?"

He didn't respond, but was quiet and I could tell something was going on. "Could you please tell me?" I said.

"I miss Daddy," he said. I was impressed that he was able to be so honest and pinpoint his feelings and recognize them and tell me about them without being guarded. I can barely do that and I'm a thirty-nine-year-old woman.

But I'll get better, and one day when Jack's potentially going to play a porn star in a biopic, I'll be that beaming mom writing a letter to an editor expressing my pride for all the world to see.

# Playing House

It would be easy to say that my first marriage was a mistake. It ended in divorce, so clearly it wasn't the best decision I ever made. But when I look back on that relationship, it barely seems real. It felt as if we were play-acting at being married. The whole thing was like a performance we were putting on. *Oh yeah, this is what married people do. They buy a car and a house.* After dating and living together, marriage seemed like the next grown-up step, and in an industry where there is so much uncertainty and instability, the trajectory of our relationship felt like something we could control.

Let me back up. Ben and I started dating when I was twenty-two. As you may remember, dear reader, we met in Seattle while filming *Lovers Lane*, and I was crushing on him, hard. After the movie we talked a bit, so I called him when I flew down to meet the man who eventually became my manager, and we hooked up the entire time. It was fun—of course it was. He was hot and was an actor and had the fancy LA life that I was in awe of.

Soon after that weekend, my manager called and asked me to fly down to audition for *Scary Movie*. I stayed at Ben's apartment, which was basically a frat house of really hot guys, and during that week I got the role of Cindy Campbell. There was an immediate shift in the power dynamic of our relationship after that, though I didn't clock it at the time. I was so dizzy with the idea of doing a movie and getting a gig, it never occurred to me that this moment of success could have a negative impact on what was then a budding relationship. Right after I booked the role, Ben and I walked into his place and he announced that I had just gotten the lead in a Wayans brothers movie, and one of his roommates looked at me and said: "Well, you got lucky." It wasn't especially kind. But now that I think about it, that shift from me being the adoring Seattle fangirl—*Oh, you go to clubs?! You have agents?!*—to suddenly having a gig and an agent of my own was probably surreal for Ben, too.

When I moved to LA for good after getting the role, Ben and I started officially dating. Four months later, we moved in together. It was sort of by accident. Ben had been living with a roommate, but things weren't going well between them so he asked if he could stay at my place. I was hesitant—it certainly felt fast—but also thrilled, because I loved him. I think we both thought living together would be temporary, but then it wasn't. I realize now, of course, that I didn't think it through, because you can't really backtrack to just dating after you live with someone, and I learned that the hard way. We bounced from apartment to apartment, and I hid the fact that we were living together from my parents for almost two years. They knew I was dating Ben. In fact, when my mom first met him she was superswoony at his looks, which only reinforced for me the idea that I should stick with this relationship. But when my parents came to visit, which wasn't nearly as often as I went to Washington, I made him stay with friends and hide his stuff and we did a whole crafty lie job. Deep down, I knew that moving in together after only four months—two of which I had spent shooting *Scary Movie* in Vancouver—was something I should keep quiet.

We lived together for a while more before getting engaged. There were six months between the proposal in the watch store and the one in the hotel. My first marriage refusal had become a big argument in our relationship, so when the second one came along, I certainly felt like I had to say yes. It's not like I wanted to date anybody else—I didn't. I loved Ben. But I also felt like I didn't have the time or the courage to be single in Los Angeles. You see, another aspect of my high defense mechanism involved never letting myself get bummed out if I didn't get a role. I wouldn't dwell on my failures or even talk about them, to Ben or to anyone. I felt like I had to keep my guard up, and being single and dating makes you vulnerable. Trying to become an actor was already terrifying enough, to add searching for a relationship and friends to that list? That felt like too much. I couldn't handle the idea of rejection in that many places at once.

And so we got engaged. You know those articles that the *New York Times* publishes every few years that list some variation of the questions you should ask your partner before you get married? Things like, "Do our ideas about spending match?" and "Will we have children?" and "If we do, will we raise them with religion?" Ben and I asked each other none of these questions. We briefly brought up kids right before getting married, and he told me he didn't want any. I explained that I couldn't marry him if that was a certainty because I didn't know what I wanted, so he agreed not to take children off the table. That was the extent of our prep for our life together.

In reading this all back, it seems clear that there were plenty of red flags in this relationship. We obviously weren't ready for marriage, at least not to each other. I've often tried to understand my rationale for getting married the first time, because it does seem baffling to commit to a lifelong relationship when there are so many glaring problems. I still wonder why I did that, and I don't fully have the answers and I don't know if I ever will. But I know that it felt like we were crossing something off the list. *Live together, check. Marriage, check.*

Listeners often call into the podcast with similar situations. They might be dating someone despite a ton of red flags—they're asking themselves questions like, *Why does this person make me feel bad? Why do I let him?*—or they're just not sure how they feel about whomever it is they're dating. In those cases, the caller usually already knows what he or she needs to do and doesn't really need to hear it from us. But back then, when Ben and I were about to get hitched, I never even let myself ask those questions. I was too proud. And the truth is that I resisted asking for any kind of help. Maybe because I was something of a loner, always the girl with only a couple of friends. But the bigger concern than my number of friends was my hesitance to confide in the friends I had. For a long time, especially in my twenties, I drove female friends away because while I loved to talk about their problems, I never wanted to divulge or confront any of my own.

My brother and I have talked about this a lot. He and I have both had failed marriages. And we were the product of a really great one. My mom and dad love each other. They get a kick out of each other. My dad still makes my mom laugh and is always telling her how beautiful she is. So on paper, it would seem that Bob and I should have had stable relationships right out of the gate. But now we've come to think that maybe it was because of the pressure we put on ourselves to check off the "happily married" box that we didn't really examine the flaws in some of our relationships as well as we should have.

It's not that our parents pressured us to get married young. Except, maybe they did. Like this one time, when I was thirteen, I told my dad that I didn't want to get married until I was twenty-seven, and he said, "Well that makes me kind of sad."

"Why, Dad?" I asked.

"Because I think you are going to want to experience intimacy before then," he said. "And Mom and I think you should wait until you are married."

My parents say they waited until they were married to have sex, and my brother and I both felt some pressure to do the same. But I think there was also a pressure into monogamy, too. That definitely contributed to my fear of being single or dating or having sexual encounters of any kind. I felt so inexperienced, and I was taught that I should want to stay that way.

(I never actually intended to wait until I was married, though. My parents eventually found out that Ben and I were living together and they ultimately had no illusions about what was going on.)

Ben and I were married for two and a half years. Our wedding was in 2004, when I was twenty-seven, and we were together until shortly after my thirtieth birthday, in 2007. It was a rough time for both of us. I was singularly focused on my career at that point, and Ben repeatedly accused me of putting my work first. I couldn't understand what he was getting at. I kept thinking, *I'm in one of the most competitive businesses in the world; if I don't put all of myself into this career I'm not going to have it.*

During the weeks just before my thirtieth birthday, people kept asking me what I was going to do to celebrate. I'd never been a big birthday person in general, but for this one I rented a great big house about three and a half hours north of LA in Paso Robles. There were eight couples, and it was a really great trip. There was a no-gifts rule, but I told everyone that I wanted them to either make something or perform something, and my friends rose to the occasion. (If there is a theme of this book, maybe it's that if we ever meet, please come prepared with song and dance.) It was a huge success and a total blast of a weekend. But I spent not one moment alone with Ben, and I noticed it. Even then I was thinking, *This is odd. I'm staying up all night talking in bed with my girlfriends, Ben is downstairs playing Ping-Pong, and I'm happy about that. Huh.*

On my actual birthday, I was hit with an odd wave of liberation. I'm not usually into those definitive age milestones, but I felt a weird sense of freedom that morning, and I think it was during that weekend that I subconsciously planted the seed that I was going to make a big transition with Ben soon.

Not long after that getaway, I was filming a movie in England, and Ben and I decided to skip Christmas with our families and spend two weeks traveling the English countryside instead. It was an amazing trip and we stayed at all these tiny inns and ate at funky cool pubs and it was great, except every day we were searching for conversation. I don't know if that had always been the case and I had just never realized it, or if it was a new development, but I felt like I was working hard at communicating with him. I barely even knew what his interests were, which perhaps speaks to my own issues of being self-absorbed. I knew he was really good at interior design and fashion—both areas that are not my strong suit, to put it mildly. It was as if I suddenly realized, after almost a decade, that we had nothing in common.

About two months after that trip, I left Ben. I have to be honest, it felt like a two-hundred-pound backpack had been taken off my shoulders. I was so exhausted from trying to make the relationship work, which I think is another reason I stayed in it so long. The thought of breaking up felt even more draining than staying together. I would think to myself, *If I kick him out of the apartment that we both signed the lease on, logistically how does that work? What's the law about that?* Fuck that. I was too tired.

That relationship ended ten years ago. And while I don't have any regrets, I certainly had some takeaways regarding how I wanted to approach my next relationship, and how I might advise others wondering about marriage, too. If I could instill one thing in my son, Jack, for example, it would be to wait until he is thirty to get married. I know that's a cynical thing to say, and I know it ruffles feathers, but for me the twenties were so much about career growth. I was working really hard and was in a selfish place. I was a much more insecure and jealous person back then, and I didn't have a lot of extra room in my life to allow for a relationship, let alone a marriage.

The best thing to come out of my first marriage, for me, was the recognition of what I want from the people in my life and what I need from those I surround myself with. People should constantly calibrate the amount of joy versus the amount of discontent a person brings them. I've eliminated, as much as I can, people who don't bring me happiness and I've realized it's not worth it for any of us to keep those people in our lives. I basically take the same approach to my social life as Marie Kondo does to a coat closet. I have a good friend in a bad relationship, for example, and I try not to get too harpy with her, but I do challenge her with this basic idea of joy all the time. "Think about this," I'll say. "Does he make you happy fifty percent of the time? Sixty percent?" No one can expect to be completely happy 100 percent of the time, but if you're spending the majority of a relationship feeling like crap because of the other person, that probably means something.

As I imagine is the case for any divorce, the failures of that relationship reverberated through my next one. My learnings from my marriage impacted who I chose to date next, and also the way I behaved with him. I'm happy to say that despite having just left a failed marriage, I was not skeptical of love or men or relationships the next time one came around—and, as you'll soon see, that happened pretty fast.

When I met Chris, the most striking thing about him was that he knew how to be happy and he knew how to make the best out of a bad day. He was constantly seeing the positive in everything. When I looked back at my marriage, and many of my relationships before it, I realized I had always equated cynicism, discontent, and anger with intelligence, and getting together with Chris made me reexamine that. It made me realize that being with someone who was well-liked and popular actually made me happy.

Still, I didn't emerge from my first marriage completely unscathed. I'm only human, and I'd just ended a relationship that, all in, spanned eight years of my life. So while I was struck by (even skeptical of) Chris's generosity of spirit, I definitely took an approach at the beginning of our relationship that could be categorized by a single mantra: "I'm not putting up with any shit anymore."

For example: When Chris and I started dating he was chronically late. One time, he said he'd be over in thirty minutes, so I decided to cook. Chicken stuffed with lemons and roasted tomatoes and a big loaf of my famous garlic bread. (Spoiler: It's famous because it's covered in butter.) After an hour of waiting for him to show, I left. I walked out of my own home and went for a long walk. I didn't want to—in fact I wanted desperately to see him—but I felt like I had spent so many years having so little power in my relationships, and I didn't want to be in a place in my life where I was constantly waiting for somebody. I had done that already, and was over it. I wanted some consideration. I had to set boundaries, because I was so wary of feeling bulldozed in any way. When Chris finally showed up at my house he called me in a panic and I told him where I was: at a restaurant on Hollywood Boulevard by myself. After that, Chris was always on time, which I acknowledge is a good argument for relationship game-play. I hate that term, but that's the reality of what I did. I liked Chris so much but I didn't want to appear overeager. I would do things like not call him back immediately—I would wait a whole (gasp!) twenty or thirty minutes because I was so proud, even though I wanted so much to hear his voice.

I think the real problem was that as soon as Chris and I

started dating, I wanted to marry him. I was head over heels, and that made me feel helpless in a period of my life when all I wanted was to feel powerful and understand my self-worth. I guess that was all part of the "divorce journey," a phrase that genuinely makes me want to throw up.

# Listener Advice:
## How to Get Over a Breakup

There's a lot I don't know about navigating relationships. I know what has worked for me, and what hasn't, but that's it. You're just as qualified as I am, dear reader, to give love advice. (Unless you're a psychologist, or a psychiatrist, or a social worker, or, I don't know, a sex expert—is that a thing?—in which case you are much *more* qualified than I am.) I'm just lucky enough to have a platform to indulge my desire to tell people what to do in their relationships. But given the knowledge that I'm totally unqualified, I wanted to gather some of your thoughts, too, so that any reader looking for actionable, helpful advice on dealing with a real problem might have a good range of tips to choose from.

So I posted this question on Facebook: *What's your best "getting over a breakup" advice? If someone called into your podcast with a broken heart, what would you tell them?*

Here's what you said:

Keep your mind busy. Dive into work, friendships, and hobbies. Don't stop to dwell on the past until you are far enough away from it to really understand what happened.

—Elec

Let yourself have a weekend to indulge your feelings, because if you tuck them away, eventually they'll resurface. Then focus on all the other kinds of love in your life and keep busy by doing something on your bucket list or taking up a new hobby. Don't try to meet anyone right away, because we all need time to heal and the next person you date deserves the best of you, not the parts of you that are still emotionally involved with your last partner.

—Courtney

Go out. Even though it sucks mostly. Make as many friends as possible. Not Facebook friends, real friends.

—Weston

---

Allow yourself to be as sad as you need to be. The more you feel your feelings, the sooner you can move through them. Some people get over it in three days of sadness and some take weeks. Stop pressuring yourself to bedone at a certain time and treat yourself with compassion!

—Natasha

---

Drink the first night ('cause let's be real). Then pamper yourself and spend time with friends and family. And eat lots of pizza.

—Katie

---

You need to go through the journey—the process of owning your responsibility in the relationship and the breakup. Be honest with yourself. At what point was there a first red flag that you ignored? And the next? And the next? When you examine that, you'll get insight. Is this a pattern? Why do I do that? What do I not value about myself that allows me to allow someone else to treat me badly? Once you do the difficult self-work, then you'll be free and ready to welcome the right partner into your life. It's neither fun nor easy to do that work, but it can be life-changing.

—Ann

Delete them from all social media! You don't need to see any of that. Take some time away from social media, too, because you'll be tempted to look and drive yourself crazy.

—Allyson

I don't think you need to dwell in the past, but I don't think you need to forget it, either. Time will do its work. There is no recipe for heartbreak, unfortunately. People who you loved will always be a part of you—you gave them your heart, so it's normal that they took a piece of it. For better or worse, they are part of your history. The only thing you can do is cherish what was good and forget about the bad. And focus on the future. Now you have a whole new opportunity to meet somebody else who will be even more awesome than your ex!

—Cassien

Get under as many people as possible.

—Dane

I'm a firm believer in exes staying exes. If you broke up, it was for a reason, and chances are they didn't suddenly change overnight. Go out, have fun, and get outside your comfort zone. Don't worry about the timeline, worry about yourself. If you feel ready to start dating a week later, go for it. No one knows you better than you.

—Dory

Be really careful about the music that you listen to during the worst part of the breakup. I have ruined some of my favorite albums because now I associate most of the songs with feeling terrible.

—Samantha

You don't just "get over" a bad breakup. You live it. You experience it. You wallow. You overanalyze.

You question what went wrong and why you weren't good enough. It took me three and a half years to get over the worst breakup of my life with the only person I've ever fully given my heart to. I experienced every feeling on every single level— hatred, anger, sadness, confusion, guilt, etc. After you experience it, you wonder how to get over it for so long that you actually are over it before you even realize. You'll look back glad that it's over and glad that you've learned from it. There's no timetable that dictates how long it takes, but it will happen.

—Kelly

I like to do something I've never done. Like go to the movies on my own, or go on a hike. It gives a sense of independence that is refreshing.

—Rebecca

Take things one day at a time. Grieve, because technically something did die, a relationship you had with a fellow human being. Do whatever you can to become a better person, whether it's pursuing deeper spirituality, taking up boxing, reading more, or meeting new people. And have at least one crazy night involving tequila.

—Bethany

---

# Take Me Home Tonight.
# Literally.

**W**hen I first met Chris, I was constantly looking for proof that he was not as great as he seemed. It was 2007, and we were in Phoenix filming *Take Me Home Tonight*, a movie about a bunch of recent college graduates in the late eighties that follows them over the course of one night. Chris and I played a couple. I was still married to Ben (it was after my thirtieth birthday weekend but before our official breakup), and even though neither of us was happy in the relationship, I was still technically off the market. All the more reason why I was skeptical of Chris's general kindness. What was in it for him?

One day I left my credit card at Kmart, and I mentioned that to Chris during shooting. He spent what felt like all day trying to track it down for me, talking to customer rep after customer rep, and requesting to speak to the managers, just to help me out. I was flabbergasted, and rather than accept that maybe this was just a good guy, I tried to analyze his motives.

What did this cute but incredibly boyish big dude want from me? Why was he doing this? I had no clue. *He can't fuck me*, I thought. *I'm married. So what is it?*

And then he kept doing nice things for me. They weren't creepy; they were just respectful. Because the movie largely takes place over one evening, the whole shoot, with the exception of one day, happened at night. After filming, Chris would walk me to my door or otherwise make sure I got home safely. It baffled me.

We became friends over the course of filming, and, I should be clear, he was having his own good time. He wasn't walking me home to get in my pants. He was hooking up with some of the cute background actresses, and I eventually started acting as his wingwoman. I loved it, and was so impressed with myself for being the cool girl who helped him hook up with hotties. But then I found myself feeling incredibly jealous of said hotties, and starting to wonder what the fuck was going on in my head. In hindsight, I was obviously crushing on him, but I don't know that I realized it at the time, even subconsciously. He was so different from anyone I'd ever been attracted to. He was kind and silly and totally beloved on set. Plus, as an actor, he was *really* good, and I was kind of taken aback by that. He was so daring and uninhibited during scenes, and I remember realizing that I was acting with someone who felt really free, and it was jarring and wonderful at the same time.

Ben came to visit me one time during the filming of that movie. I ended up going home early, but everyone else— including Ben—went to a club, and he came crawling home from his wild night out at about 7:00 A.M. I don't know what exactly went down, but the next evening I was talking with Topher Grace, who played my brother in the film. "Anna, what the fuck are you doing with that guy?" he asked me. It was such a wonderful cold splash of water in the face. People had hedged around the idea that we weren't right for each other before, but that dancing-around-the-issue approach made me defensive. Nobody had just come out and said it like that.

I thought about the question for a moment, looked him in the eye, and answered. "I don't know," I said.

The whole cast was staying in some dumpy apartment complex, and a few nights later Chris invited a bunch of us to his apartment to hang out and eat elk Rice-A-Roni, made with elk that he'd hunted and brought with him from Salt Lake City. It was a fun evening, and Chris and I were at our peak banter. Though we didn't act on it physically, I couldn't deny that something was happening between us. The next day I went to my friend Dan Fogler, a really talented actor and costar of the film, and confided in him that I wanted to leave my husband and I didn't know what to do.

"I saw you and Chris last night, and it was like I was watching Ping-Pong," he said. (He starred in *Balls of Fury*, a Ping-Pong movie that came out that year, so it was top of mind.) "You two were so into each other."

Dan also told me that if I was going to leave my husband, I had to be a surgeon with a scalpel about it. Do it immediately and effectively, he said. So I called Ben and told him over the phone that I was leaving him, and then went to set and was like, "Hey, everybody! I just left my husband." Pretty soon I was knocking on Chris's door and was basically like, "Hi. I'm ready to get boned."

I know that leaving your husband over the phone is a questionable decision, and I definitely felt like the villain in that moment. But as I've mentioned, a real part of the reason I didn't break up with Ben sooner was that the prospect of it just sounded so exhausting. Dealing with all the broken pieces of our relationship was daunting enough that I basically put it off until I couldn't anymore. And in an odd way, we'd been through so much together at that point that it felt like the only way to do it. Had I told him face-to-face, not only would I have had to wait longer, but it would have been hor- rible drama.

Breaking the news from afar was, in some ways, the easy way out. I won't deny that. But even on the phone I had to repeat myself a number of times before he took me at my word. "You're just tired; you're really tired," he responded at first. I just said, "Nope, I'm leaving you." And that was that.

The end of the relationship was long overdue. We hadn't been happy for a while, but the reality is that if I hadn't met Chris, my first marriage probably would have lasted until I found a different someone else. Chris was my cattle prod. I needed someone to come along and show me something dif- ferent than the relationship I knew, even if he did so without realizing it. I wish I could have figured that out on my own, but I didn't. It probably has to do with the public proclamation of marriage and my incredible reluctance to admit failure. Basically, my pride mixed with my what–did–I–do–wrong guilt was pretty hard to overcome.

In the moment after I broke the news to the cast and crew, Chris and I exchanged a brief glance, and we both knew what it meant. When we finally got together, it was hot and heavy in a way that I'd never experienced before. I felt a little bit guilty, mostly because I didn't want him to feel like I was pressuring him to be in a relationship with me, like, *This is what you have to do because I left my husband.*

It was extremely important to me, especially toward the end of my relationship with Ben, not to sleep with anybody while we were together. I have complicated feelings about that now. Not that I think I should have cheated on him, but I realize that that moral stance was basically a way to let myself off the hook. I think about my motivation during that time period, and I think I was looking for something to hang my hat on. Sure, I get to proclaim I didn't fuck Chris before I left Ben, but what is there to celebrate in that? It didn't make me a hero. After all, I wanted to. Desperately. And I had feelings for him, obviously, even if I wasn't honest with myself about what those were. So while I didn't cheat, I'm not completely innocent, either.

(If someone called into the podcast asking if she should leave her husband for a hot actor she hadn't slept with but already had an emotional connection with, I would totally call her out, so I can't give myself a total pass. Damn podcast.)

Chris and I grew closer over the rest of the shoot. You might think that, fresh off an almost decade-long relationship, I would be hesitant to move on to the next, but I couldn't have fallen more headfirst into my feelings for Chris.

The relationship felt so different than my previous ones. It was laughter all the time. On one of our first dates, we were in a restaurant and Chris swatted at a fly. It was on the table and still kind of partially moving so I grabbed it and popped it in my mouth and ate it. It was weird and gross and impulsive but spoke to that part of me that indulgently wants to freak people out. I was taking a gamble that it would pay off and he'd be impressed, and it paid off. I think I was also trying to prove that I was a soldier, and that I wasn't afraid of anything. I take pride in not being a high-maintenance person, which is probably exactly the kind of thing a high-maintenance person would say.

From doing the podcast, I've come to learn that guys like to come to the rescue. On one of our episodes, I asked Sim if he was turned on by girls who know a lot about sports (Sim is a sports nut). He said no, and then went on to say that what actually turns him on is getting to educate women about sports, and of course that makes sense. I was frustrated with myself for not coming to that conclusion on my own, because I think a lot of men really do like that "Oh, I'm helpless, will you save me?" personality trait. That's a quality I don't have— I'm too proud to play the damsel in distress. Instead I eat a half-dead fly and then I'm like, "Wanna make out?"

After filming was over, Chris and I got a rental car and

drove back to LA from Phoenix together with all my shit. Upon returning, I had a lot to deal with in terms of ending my marriage. So I slept on a friend's couch, wore the same clothes every day, and got rides from Chris because Ben had our car. My life was pretty bizarre at the time, and, in terms of my relationship with Chris, I was on high alert. There was all the baggage from my marriage, but I'd also seen Chris hook up with a handful of people on our set, and I knew some of the people he had dated in the past. The point is, I had my guard up.

Still, we moved fast. I think that's just the way I'm programmed. I like to know where things are going. I need the security, and hate having questions unanswered. So when it comes to guys, I like assurance that they're in it. I like being certain of the goal. I guess that's why I didn't date much, and was never very good at it. I'm too desperate for answers.

That need for a clearly defined relationship is likely to blame for one of the more awkward interactions in my life, which came only a few months into dating Chris. Before we got together, he had planned a month-long backpacking trip through Europe with his friends and costars from the TV show *Everwood*. A month or so before he left, I was already irrationally resentful of the trip. I think it was partly because he had never called me his girlfriend before. I had no promise from him that things would pick up again when he got back. I knew Chris was crazy about me, and I was crazy about him, and he called all the time and we spent every night together, but we'd never officially used the boyfriend/girlfriend labels.

When he left, I felt abandoned. I was lonely, and pissed off he didn't call me his girlfriend, and I was starting to wonder if maybe he was just a player. Thus began that very brief period of time where I said, "Fuck it. I'm just going to screw my way through Hollywood." I didn't, though. I went to some parties and awkwardly asked guys out, but I didn't have the language to actually be romantically savvy. I would say, "Do you want to go out with me?" And when the guy said, "What?" I'd say, "What about your friend?"

So one night, while Chris was away and I hadn't talked to him in a couple of days, I went to a party and met a cute lawyer who worked in the district attorney's office. We seemed to hit it off, and a few days later, I invited him to meet me for a drink. I had never successfully asked anyone out before, but I figured that Chris was in Europe probably hooking up with other people, so I should be doing the same, if only in LA. Of course, I didn't actually want to, deep down. It wasn't like this lawyer and I had an especially magical moment. I was just trying to build a wall to protect myself against the hurt that I saw coming.

When the lawyer showed up for our date, I didn't even recognize him. We'd met on a really dark rooftop and this was a really light restaurant, and I think I was more focused on myself than I was on him during that first meeting. But we had a drink and he drove me home and I invited him in for a nightcap. The whole time I was thinking about Chris, but the lawyer came in and I went in for the kill: "So do you want to have sex with me?" I asked, not seductively at all.

To his credit, the lawyer said, "You know, I think we've had too much to drink. Can I call you tomorrow?"

"Ugh, fine," I said, pissed off that this guy wasn't jumping at the opportunity to take advantage of me.

The next day, Chris called me from a train to Prague. I could tell there were girls in the background and I was boiling with anger at the idea that he would talk to me while he was having his fun with some probably impossibly sophisticated European ladies. Or maybe they were some cool hippie Americans who actually enjoy backpacking through Europe. Either way, I wasn't having it.

But then, seemingly out of nowhere, he said, "I just love you so much. I just want to marry you."

Needless to say, I never talked to the lawyer again.

I like to think that subconsciously I was interested in that specific guy because in my heart of hearts I knew that he wouldn't really have sex with me, even when I offered. I could have picked an easier target if I really wanted to get laid, but I think there was a subconscious reason that I chose to flirt with someone who was so incredibly practical. Or is that called ethical?

When Chris got home I finally broached the issue of our labels.

"Are we doing this?" I asked. "Can I introduce you as my boyfriend?"

He looked at me like I had three heads. "Yeah, of course," he said, and I was hit with a wave of guilt. I thought Chris wasn't calling me his girlfriend intentionally. That he was being noncommittal. But it was more that we weren't being social. We never did anything where the opportunity to call me his girlfriend presented itself. We were just having sex and making each other food all the time.

Chris and I moved in together after nine months of dating. I guess I really like to jump in there! But living with Chris was an entirely different experience. He was so low-maintenance. After my divorce, I couldn't sell my house, so I had to essentially rebuy it from Ben. I was pretty broke but I was excited to move back in, and Chris's lease was up, so I suggested we live together.

"Does it bother you at all that I lived here with my ex?" I asked him once.

"No, not really," he said, and even though I think it actually did, his was a really generous answer. Still, it was a relief to both of us when we bought our new place a couple of years later. There was a feeling of joint ownership, like we were starting a new phase as a team.

It was kind of Chris to not make me feel guilty that we lived in my old house. It was similar to when I asked him if he was bothered by the fact that I was married before and he said, unsurprisingly, the perfect thing.

"Baby, you were just chilling on ice."

# Turning the Tables:
# Deal Breakers

When we do the "Deal Breakers" segment on the podcast, I'm always surprised by the things that some people say they'd put up with in a romantic partner—and, on the flip side, the things that some people just won't tolerate. Cassie Daniels, a segment producer for *Unqualified*, presented me with some deal breakers. It's a good, and bizarre, exercise in introspection.

*If a guy shaves his legs—is that a deal breaker?*

**Anna:** Why does he shave his legs?

**Cassie:** Purely aesthetic. He doesn't like the look of hair.

**Anna:** Does he not like hair on me as well?

**Cassie:** Well, he hopes you shave, too.

**Anna:** I'm going to say deal breaker. I worry this leads into other high-maintenance issues. I love weirdness in a guy, but this could be a gateway behavior. And is there a lot of hair that gets stuck in the drain? And

what if he uses my razor? That would be annoying.
I'd wonder why he doesn't do laser. I think the
shaving would probably be about some insecurities
that are bigger than just leg hair, so I'd try to say,
"It's okay, you can embrace the hair." But I don't
have the energy to build anyone's confidence
right now.

*You're dating a guy and you're on one of your first dates. You go back
to his place after a lovely evening, and he shows you his desk with
electrical parts on it and tells you he is building a time machine.
Then he looks deep into your eyes and asks you if you'll come with
him when he's ready. Deal breaker?*

**Anna:** Not a deal breaker. This is a really interesting
person. It might not be the person I marry, but I
think I would have a lot of follow-up questions.
The most obvious one would be where would you
go first?

**Cassie:** He'd go to 1973.

**Anna:** Why?

**Cassie:** He just thinks it was really an interesting time.
People were so much more open. He loved the
energy.

**Anna:** Does he like *Back to the Future*?

**Cassie:** Loves it. Huge fan. It's his favorite movie.

**Anna:** Hmmm. On the page, he sounds like an interesting
person. But now I'm worried that the conversation
is going to go a little stale. I guess I would ask him,

"Do you really believe in this? That we are truly traveling back in time?"

Cassie: "Well, there are a lot of doubters," he'd say. "But you can't let doubters stop you from achieving your dreams. But we don't have to stay there for longer than a year."

Anna: Oh, we're going long-term?

Cassie: Yeah, it's awhile.

Anna: Can we go to the future? Because as a woman there aren't a lot of times I want to go back to.

Cassie: He doesn't have that technology.

Anna: How much time does he spend on his time machine?

Cassie: All the time he's not with you.

Anna: I take it back. Deal breaker. That's too much time spent on the time machine.

Cassie: Could you be friends?

Anna: Sure. He'd be my curious friend who is into the 1970s. I would take a day trip up the coast to Hearst Castle with him.

Cassie: But nothing romantic?

Anna: I don't know. I *would* be interested to see what he's like as a lover, maybe. If we were friends and there was a little hookup, I'd be interested to see what a time-traveling man was up to in bed. And I like that he picked 1973. Maybe he's a generous lover. So we'd take an overnighter and stay at a roadside inn and talk about his vast knowledge of history. You know what? Okay, I take it back. I'm a curious person—not a deal breaker.

*You're having sex with a guy, let's call him Alex, and during the deed he calls you by his sister's name. Deal breaker?*

**Anna:** What's his sister's name?

**Cassie:** Julie.

**Anna:** Oh boy, this is a tough one. I don't think I would immediately stop, because I'm not good with surprises like that. I think in my head I'd be thinking, *Did I hear that correctly?* As opposed to stopping and asking, "Did you just call me by your sister's name?" I hate to say this, I wish that I could feel comfortable enough to ask him about it afterward, but I feel like I might ask my friends what to do. Do I really like this guy?

**Cassie:** Yeah you like him a lot. But it's still new.

**Anna:** Then maybe I would have to ask him afterward— and I would be supertentative about it, because if I really liked him I would want to believe that I heard him wrong, even if it were superaudible. As we're cleaning up—in the postcoital—I'd say, "Hey, I feel like you said Julie when we were having sex. Did I hear you correctly?

**Cassie:** He's going to tell you, "You did. I was really embarrassed, and wasn't sure if you heard it. I was talking to my sister earlier, and we've been arguing a lot so she's been on my mind."

**Anna:** "Has that ever happened before?"

**Cassie:** "No, never."

**Anna:** "It was a little jarring for me. I've never called out my *brother's* name after sex."

**Cassie:** "I don't want to have sex with her. She's just in my head right now."

**Anna:** "Yeah, it's weird how during sex the rational parts of your brain shut off. But, it threw me a little bit."

**Cassie:** "I'm only attracted to you. Not my sister."

**Anna:** "That's probably good. Thank you."

**Cassie:** "Are we good?"

**Anna:** "Yeah. You know, truthfully, I'm working really hard at being straightforward with people, so I'll just say that I kind of need to digest this for a minute."

**Cassie:** "I feel like you're being really judgmental."

**Anna:** "I don't mean to be, this is just new for me."

**Cassie:** "If you want, I could call my sister and she could explain that there's nothing sexual between us."

**Anna:** "No, I believe you. I don't need to call Julie, I just need a minute. Let's take a minute and chat in a bit." And then I would leave and call you, Cassie. If he has a lot of other great qualities I think I would give it a one-time pass. It would be weird and I'd never forget it, but if it happened a second time I would definitely be like, "I'm confused and can't get over it." My personal rule is no names during sex. It's such a deliberate thing to use a name. Like, *Okay,*

*I'm going to call him Alex now.* I'm trying to shut
down that part of my brain during sex.

Cassie: What about if he cried after sex?

Anna: I would find it fascinating but I don't think I would
judge him on it. I would tell my friends about Julie
but I wouldn't about the crying. That feels cruel.

Cassie: What about if he cried every time?

Anna: Then I would tell a trusted friend and ask if they
could guide me on it. Maybe it's just part of his
release. Who knows, maybe he would make me cry
more. That's one of my goals this year. People talk
about what a good release crying is, and it's really
hard for me to let myself go to that place.

*You are dating a guy who is over thirty and you find out he's never
been in a long-term relationship. Deal breaker?*

Anna: Well, I'm going to ask him why. If we're at that
place where we're talking about previous
relationships, I'd probably say, "Do you mind my
asking why? Is it because you don't want one? Have
you moved a lot?"

Cassie: "No, I really want one."

Anna: "Do you date all similar types of people?"

Cassie: "No, I've dated all types of people; I can just tell
quickly if we don't click."

Anna: "Really? How can you tell?"

Cassie: "It's an energy thing. Sometimes you just don't click.
Like you don't have the same movie interests . . ."

**Anna:** This is a deal breaker. He seems way too critical.
This is why I wonder a lot about online dating
where you do things like profile matches.
Because, on the page, Chris and I are extremely
different. He likes to watch sports and hunt, and
my hobbies are hiking and reading. He likes
country music, I like indie. But those are such
superficial things and don't represent the bigger
picture. It seems like this guy is looking for
excuses to say the relationship won't work. I
remember talking to a woman in LA who was
single and attractive and in her late thirties, and
she said that a guy on a date ate off her plate and
she was like, "I could never." I felt like that was a
really high bar. Even if something like that irks
you, it shouldn't be your takeaway. After talking to
this guy, I'd feel like I was under a microscope.
What if I did something wrong? Like my tube
socks—I wear tube socks. Maybe those are a big
no-no for him. And during sex I would be
especially nervous. It would make my head spin a
little bit.

*The guy you're dating tells you that when he gets married he wants to
take his wife's last name. Deal breaker?*

**Anna:** Does he hate his name?

**Cassie:** No, he just likes the idea of honoring his wife's
roots. It's really important to him.

**Anna:** That's cool. It feels a little grandiose, though. Like, *thank you*? Seems a bit like him volunteering to get my name tattooed on his arm. I don't need that. It's not a deal breaker, but it's mildly amusing, I guess. I would wonder what else would sprout out of this. Where would this desire manifest itself in other parts of his life? It *would* be a deal breaker at this point in my life if a guy insisted I take *his* name. But I think the problem with this guy is that he might be too serious for me. It seems like he is trying to prove something, like, *Look how progressive I am.* I don't have the energy for that. I might have in college, but not now. It also might indicate that he doesn't have the best sense of humor. I need a guy I can laugh with.

*During your first time having sex, the guy you just started dating turns on the TV and tells you he can only climax while watching* The Golden Girls, *in particular scenes with Bea Arthur. Deal breaker?*

**Anna:** Is it on his DVR?

**Cassie:** He has Hulu all queued up.

**Anna:** I love *The Golden Girls* but this is a deal breaker. I would hope that I knew an ex of his so I could mine her for information, but yeah, that seems like a forever hurdle. And also, not to be gossipy, but if I continued that relationship I couldn't tell that story to my friends and I would really want to tell

that story to my friends. If he was a fantastic guy
and I really loved everything else about him maybe
I would dig around eBay for something
autographed by Bea Arthur to give him as a gift
when we broke up.

# Just Friends:
## A Conversation Between a Man and a Woman Who've Been Pals for Fifteen Years and Haven't Slept Together

*My podcast partner, Sim Sarna, is more than just a producer and the willing recipient of a constant barrage of "fuck you, Sim." He's also a longtime friend. We go back over a decade, and it's always been platonic. Here's our take on how that's possible.*

**Anna:** Any conversation about our friendship has to start by addressing your bowel problems on our first couples' vacation.

**Sim:** Yes, that's true. And your advice to me was, "Next time you go on any vacation with a group of people, eat a bunch of Pepto or Imodium before you go." You said, "Stock up on those and you'll be fine. Your body will be backed up and feel awful for a week, but you won't have the runs."

**Anna:** That's how you know you've reached the pinnacle of friendship, when you can have that conversation. But for us—and correct me if I'm wrong—but for us to get to that point took time. We've known each other for years, so now the flaws we see in each other—shit-related or otherwise—have just become part of the package.

**Sim:** Well, here's the thing, Anna. You and I are very similar people, so we can handle the flaws we see in each other because they are the same ones we see in ourselves.

**Anna:** Yes, that's true. Is that why we hit it off so quickly? Maybe this is where we get into slightly dangerous territory, and I don't know if you remember it the same way I do, but even though I was in a relationship when we met, I remember being completely drawn to you. Not necessarily in a supersexual way, but I remember thinking, *Oh, he's handsome, he's interesting.* I think over time we really have developed a rare thing in that we are both straight and have a really healthy friendship that hasn't revolved around anything sexual. And for that to stay intact for more than fifteen years, that's a really long time anywhere, but especially in Hollywood.

**Sim:** Completely rare. It doesn't happen! When I first met you, I remember thinking, *Oh my God, she's so sweet and so funny.* And very attractive, obviously, but you were dating Ben at the time. I was drawn to you, though, because no one had ever made me laugh that hard. You were so funny.

**Anna:** Really? Go on.

**Sim:** Not only were you funny, but you were self-deprecating and you were . . . you were you! Everyone wanted to be around you, and I did, too. I thought you were incredible.

**Anna:** It's so true. I am. But seriously, I found your intelligence and wit so refreshing. I instantly liked you better than all the other new people I was meeting. At the time I was new to LA and you were one of my very first friends. I was still compiling a social network, and I think we had a little bit of a kismet thing that I couldn't quite put my finger on.

**Sim:** Do you remember the first time we met? It was at Le Colonial, at the corner of Beverly and Robertson. I remember because there was a lounge above the restaurant and it was the hot spot for like two or three weeks. In LA, there's always the hot new place and this was it for a brief moment in January 2001.

**Anna:** I totally remember. You knew one of the producers of *Scary Movie* and he invited me to go out with a bunch of his friends, and we all started hanging out as a group for a while. But I'm not friends with any of the others anymore. Not because anything bad happened, just . . . time.

Sim: Yeah, but those were our friends for a long while. Today, I'm Facebook friends with all of them but it's been years since I've actually spoken to any of them.

Anna: Oh, I need to grill you on some of this, because I have no idea where they've been. I'm not so active on Facebook.

Sim: That's interesting. I hadn't thought of that until now, that you have zero connection to them since you're barely on Facebook. For me, if they like a picture of mine on social media, I think, *Wow, after fifteen years they are still in my life*. But that's all it is, just a like on Facebook. Meanwhile, you probably haven't thought of them in years. Like if you saw our old friend Eddie, you'd be like, "Holy shit, I used to hang out with you every day and I now haven't seen you in ten years."

Anna: Yeah, probably. Or I'd be like, "Sorry, what's your name again?" No, I'm kidding. I don't mean to sound like such a bitch. But there are a lot of transitional people in Hollywood.

Sim: That's true.

Anna: Which is why it's so cool, and unusual, that we're still friends. Navigating heterosexual friendship is tricky, and that was especially true when we were in our twenties and all of us were putting on a bit of an act. Yet you always had something more to offer. I think we understood each other's sense of humor and, this might sound selfish, but you had more to offer me, personality-wise, than a lot of the other new people I was meeting.

Sim: That's so nice of you to say.

Anna: But really, as I think more about it, maybe the reason our friendship has worked is as simple as the fact that, Sim, you're not a fucking creep.

Sim: Yup. That's pretty much what it comes down to. But I'll admit, I had a really rough time, especially at the beginning of our friendship, because you were in a relationship and the three of us became close and I felt third-wheely a lot. It was strange to have a relationship with two people who I figured would be together for life, yet I clearly wanted to spend my time with one over the other.

Anna: Me?

Sim: Absolutely not.

Anna: I figured. But it's true—we've seen each other through so many relationships. Well, I've seen you through a few more than you have me, but not many. You're a monogamist like I am.

Sim: True. I haven't had that many girlfriends.

Anna: I'm so grateful that Chris doesn't have that many female friends. I have some girlfriends in long-term relationships where their male partners have a lot of female friends and, I don't know, it's tough. Is it a completely archaic idea that men can't have female friends? I mean, you have me.

Sim: Yeah, I hear what you're saying. I'm pretty sure that every one of my fiancée Amy's guy friends wants to sleep with her, so I understand feeling hesitant about your partner's relationships.

Anna: Totally.

Sim: But seriously, every single one. Even the ones who are married with kids!

Anna: Is that because men are selfish in friendship? Do they think they're not getting anything out of a relationship with a woman if they can't even entertain the idea of scoring? Or what? What is it, Sim? Why don't most men like being friends with women? Speak for all mankind, please.

Sim: I don't know. I'm a guy and I'm friends with you. But even in our case, we've had a platonic friendship for so long, and it has still been hard for some people. My ex-wife had an issue with it.

Anna: She did not care for me at all.

Sim: She didn't. She seemed threatened by our relationship, which is why you and I were out of touch for years. I was so glad you were at my wedding, but then we only saw each other a couple of times over the next two years while my marriage was crumbling.

Anna: I wasn't mad at you for that, because I understood, but I hated that when I did see you, you didn't seem very happy. Of course, I wasn't totally innocent in that. I think that at least on a subconscious level I kind of knew that she wasn't digging me, so maybe I put a bit more attention into killing her with kindness. But I never wanted to stress her out or put her down. I always wanted to treat her well.

Sim: You tried. I was so disappointed that she was threatened by you because you really did try.

Anna: She probably thought the same way I do, in a lot of ways. That if a guy is going to be friends with a gal, usually he is at least partially thinking about getting laid.

Sim: Yeah, sure, for some guys that's the case. But I've never really been like that. I've always been comfortable with women as friends. I was such a late bloomer that when I would talk to girls or become friends with them, even in college, I just knew I had no chance with them.

Anna: Oh, Sim.

Sim: No, it's true, and it's fine. And it made it so that girls could get to know me and see me as a friend. I was always the friend guy, and I didn't mind it so much. In my twenties, I began to gain a little more confidence with women, but at the heart of it I'm still a really shy guy who doesn't think he has a chance with most girls, so he's lucky to be friends with them.

Anna: You just tapped into something that I think is crucially important, which is that we were both late bloomers. And because of that, we approached every interaction with a "this person does not want to fuck me" attitude. In an odd way, that is a very fundamental common bond that contributes to everything we do. Maybe that's how we were able to maintain this friendship for so long. Because neither one of us would ever think someone wanted to screw us. There! We've figured out the secret to men and women being friends. Be people who were awkward in childhood.

Sim: Totally. When people ask me if men and women can be friends, I say yes. But I have to caveat that with the fact that, again, it's rare. Not necessarily winning the lottery rare, but winning the raffle at a carnival rare. Your odds are low, but there's a chance.

Anna: But then what happens when one of you enters a relationship?

Sim: The same thing we did with Amy. When she and I started dating, she had to contend with the fact that there was another woman who consumed my life. Someone who, because she's my business partner, I think about every hour of the workday and I am hearing her voice in my ear, literally, all the time—

Anna: And she's an obnoxious actress . . .

Sim: And she's an obnoxious actress! Amy entered our relationship already feeling like the other woman, so it was difficult at the beginning. But I was totally up front with her about my relationship with you—which is now both a personal friendship and a professional partnership—and she's been just amazing. And, certainly, it's a credit to you that you've gone out of your way to make her feel comfortable.

Anna: That's kind of you to credit me, but she's been great. She's more confident than any woman I've seen you with, so when I reach out to her independently of you, she's completely engaged. She and I have a nice friendship, and it was important to me that she felt safe with the time that you and I spend together. There's nothing weird going on; we're just trying to make this silly podcast and we'll see what happens. But really, to her credit, she heard that. She registered what I had to say. If I were in Amy's shoes, I don't know if I could have dealt with it very well, or at all. I would have been like, "Fuck this."

Sim: She was very mature about the whole thing, and I think that's a part of it. Every day that I spend working on the podcast is partly because I want to create a life with her, and she's so proud of me—and of us—that it makes me continue to work harder.

Anna: That is really sweet. Obviously it's different with Chris and me because we've known each other for a decade. But you were in my life when he and I met.

Sim: I met him before you did!

Anna: Oh yeah, I forgot about that. Why do I forget anything that's not about me?

Sim: We weren't friends or anything, but I had met him socially before.

Anna: I will say that after we started the podcast Chris said to me, "So is Sim like your best friend now?" It wasn't an accusation. There was no undertone of "Are you sleeping with him?" or any kind of allusion to anything sexual, but it was a vulnerable moment on his part because you and I were spending so much time together. It was sweet, though. I loved that he was missing my company. On one hand, Chris is incredibly impressed by the fact that you and I just talked about creating this thing a couple of years ago and now it is actually happening. On the other hand, this is more time away from family life. And that will be the constant struggle of all our lives. But it was of comfort to me that he said that. I would have been really bummed if he was like, "No, talk to Sim as long as you want. Do whatever you want. I'm fine." It's always nice when someone wants to be around you.

Sim: Everyone wants to be around you. Why do you think so many people agreed to do our podcast back when it was new and unkown? People love to hang out with you.

Anna: Fuck you, Sim.

# Scoliosis Check

**E**ach year of middle school, there was one day where we had no choice but to reveal our bodies to the other girls in the grade. That day was scoliosis-check day. I was incredibly flat-chested in middle school. I got a training bra long before I needed it, just because everyone else had one, and I got made fun of—a lot—for my lack of boobs. Most days, even in the locker room before gym, you didn't have to take your shirt off in front of anyone. You could just do that maneuver where you put one shirt on before taking the other one off and—poof!—you were in your gym clothes. But for scoliosis check, you had to line up in your bra and wait to bend over so the nurse could check your spine. It was the longest wait ever. I couldn't have been flatter, and I was sure the other girls were all quietly assessing my completely lacking body.

Scoliosis-check day was not a fun day.

To the extent that I developed at all—I never grew to be

very tall and certainly didn't wake up as a C cup one day—it happened relatively late. In high school, I could have easily been cast as one of the geeks in *Freaks and Geeks*. I had no boobs, no curves, and I wanted those things desperately. My classmates used to talk about "being on the rag" or "getting a visit from Aunt Flo," and I had no idea what they were talking about. I seriously believed, *Okay, I guess this isn't going to happen for me. I'm going to be one of those girls whose period just doesn't come.* I finally got it when I was fifteen.

During my junior year of high school, I went through a small growth spurt and put on a little bit of weight—enough to distinguish myself from a fifth-grade boy, at least—and by senior year there were a couple of times when I actually started to feel more attractive. One day this guy Shane looked at me and said, "Man, you've really grown up, Faris." And despite the fact that I probably should have been disgusted, instead I was like, *No way! Could I be attractive?* That was a really exciting idea for me, even though I didn't really buy into it. "Hot girl" has never been an identity that I've been fully comfortable with. Even if I'm in hot pants and my hair and makeup are done and I'm playing a character who feels hot, I just can't embrace it. And that's not because I think I'm unattractive or anything. I just think you have to take yourself really seriously to identify as hot, and to this day I have too much wrapped up in the idea of being the incredibly insecure fifteen-year-old who nobody wants to hook up with. I think that identity will forever be a part of me, and I don't really mind.

Like all women, I also remember the day I realized that my weight would always be a point of discussion. When I was thirteen, I was at a coffee shop with my friend and her mom, and I ordered a hot chocolate with whipped cream.

"Are you sure you want whipped cream with that?" my friend's mom asked me.

That was a mile marker for me. It was the first time I thought, *Oh fuck, am I not supposed to get the whipped cream?* (As for the mom, like most adults who have no idea how impactful their supposedly innocuous comments are, she probably thought nothing of it. She was desensitized.) It really threw me, and I felt so ashamed. I didn't finish my hot chocolate or eat the whipped cream in the end, because I immediately thought I must be fat or was going to get fat.

Overall, though, my body image stuff has been much more about my face and breasts than my body size. I never had a crazy obsession with weight. It's probably only third or fourth on my list of body image issues. First comes face, particularly lips, then breasts, then weight, then hands.

And yes, it's sad that I can cite a list, and that I can guarantee that all women have these lists. I was about to write that I can't imagine a man having a similar list, but I don't know. Living in Hollywood I've definitely been around some vain men, a number of whom have been unattractively obsessed with how they look or what they weigh or how much hair they've lost, which is actually really comforting to us women at the end of the day. At least dudes have their own stuff they beat themselves up about.

Self-obsession is more commonplace in today's world of selfies, too. It's more socially acceptable to be at once insecure and vain about looks, no matter your gender.

So anyway, let's run down the list, shall we?

## #1. LIPS.

I have a scar on my upper lip from a bike accident I had with my brother, and I always had thin lips anyway. So around the time that I was filming *The House Bunny*, I started getting injections in my upper lip. I did it for a little bit and I noticed a small difference, but no one else ever said anything. I kept wondering if anybody else even noticed. Turned out, after doing it long enough, the injections became very apparent. One day a bunch of my friends were like, "Hey, Anna, your lips are getting pretty big." At that point, I had to wean myself off the injections. In the world of Angelina Jolie, who doesn't want big, puffy beautiful lips? But I look back at the decision to get injections as a mistake. Not because I judge other people for doing it—I really don't—but because it definitely wasn't the right choice for me.

## #2. BOOBS.

My breasts were a huge point of insecurity from an early age. By the time I reached my twenties, I finally felt confident enough in my body to accept that little breasts could be sexy, too. I was finally starting to own them—wearing skimpy tops and telling myself I could get away with certain outfits because without cleavage I didn't feel boobalicious, which I acknowledge is crazy thinking in its own right. But around age thirty, my breasts started sinking into my chest a little more, and instead of being the tiniest perky boobs, they started to be the tiniest saggy boobs.

The idea of getting a boob job sprung, initially, from my work on *The House Bunny*. (Not to pin all my plastic surgery on that project but . . .) Before shooting that movie, in which I played a Playboy Bunny turned sorority house mom, I had never had attention drawn to my chest, ever. But with the outfits in *The House Bunny*, it was hard to look away. At first I was incredibly uncomfortable with the attention. I'd come to the set of two hundred people and think, *Holy shit, everyone is looking at my boobs.* Plus, my nipples were constantly popping out of the heavily, heavily, *heavily* padded bra that they sewed me into every day. It was embarrassing, until it wasn't. After, like, day five, I started thinking the attention wasn't so bad. In fact, it was kind of cool. Maybe I was becoming more like my character, but I started to embrace her kind of sexuality and it was really liberating.

At the same time, I was dating Chris. I feel silly saying this, but he brought out something in me that made me want to be feminine in a very traditional way. But I also wanted to be independent. So, one night, I turned to him and said, "I think I'm going to get breast implants."

"Honey, I love your body no matter what you do," he said. Perfect answer.

Other guys had talked to me about getting implants in the past, and I hated that so much. It would piss anyone off, I think, to hear the people who supposedly love you suggest that you should get surgery to change your body. It automatically implies that your current looks aren't good enough. So if you come up with it on your own, all you want to hear from the person you love is, "You're beautiful no matter what."

For a long time, I really thought that getting a boob job defined a person. The woman who would get implants was a specific type of person and that person was not me. That person was weak and frivolous and fake and all the things that I felt I wasn't, which is what makes it particularly ironic that I ended up electing for the surgery.

I did it for myself. I wasn't doing it for Hollywood—I'd been wearing padded bras for my whole career, so it wasn't like I thought that implants were going to suddenly help me get ahead. But I wanted to feel sexy in a way that I hadn't been feeling, and, I'll be honest, after getting the surgery, I did. It was really fun. I know it sounds dumb to describe plastic surgery as fun, but to be able to fill out a bikini for the first time in my life, that really was exciting. I'd recently ended my first marriage and I was clearly going through a year of revolutionary change—independence and a boob job!

The doctor I went to was great. He encouraged me to make only the most modest change that would still give me the look I was going for. Before I had the operation he said to me, "Listen, I want to see you a year from now and I want you to say, 'I wish we had gone bigger.'" That's when you know your implant doctor is really looking out for your best interests.

Unlike the lips, I have no regrets about getting breast implants. I'm happy I did it, but I'm happy that I waited until I was thirty. It's a personal decision, and I certainly wouldn't recommend it to everyone. But it does bother me that women are very much criticized by other women for these kinds of choices. They are, admittedly, dramatic ones—luxurious, perhaps even frivolous, decisions that require you to go under the knife so you can have bigger boobs or a bigger butt. But I don't know why we're quite so hard on each other about it. My harshest criticism has come from women. On one hand, I do understand that drastic body change is conforming to a male ideal. But on the other hand, I've been bleaching my hair since I was fourteen. I had braces. I whitened my teeth. It's not exactly the same, but there is an element of line drawing—who gets to say what we can or cannot do for vanity?

### #3. MOVING ON TO WEIGHT . . .

I've always been a fairly small person, so weight hasn't been my focal point when it comes to looks. But you can't be a woman in America, let alone in Hollywood, and not maintain a general undercurrent of awareness that your weight is subject to constant scrutiny. It's virtually impossible to drown that out entirely. When I moved to LA, I was really thin. I had just graduated from college, so I'd been living on a dining hall food plan. I didn't eat particularly well, but I didn't eat much, either, and I walked everywhere. Probably seven or eight miles a day. So when I arrived in LA, I wasn't panicked about weight. Not about weight, but about basically everything else.

I did gain a lot of weight with my pregnancy, and I've never had more paparazzi follow me. I knew why, of course. I was on the bump watch. At the time, I honestly didn't give a fuck, probably because my brain was numb with pregnancy hormones and I was in a blissful state and all I wanted to do was eat. Food had never tasted so delicious. I mean, food was always good, but when I was pregnant it took on a whole new power. So, even though Jack was born about two months early, I gained seventy pounds. At around six months pregnant, my doctor was like, "Okaaaaay, you're gaining a lot of weight pretty quickly." But it felt so good to not think about it, which makes me wonder if maybe all along I'd been worrying about weight more than I thought. Maybe the seed had been planted so young that it was woven into the fabric of my psyche without my realizing it. Probably.

I wish I had good advice for how to not absorb the weight pressure. Maybe one of you dear readers can teach me. All I know is that I can't stand comments about weight. Even complimenting someone on losing weight, it's always uncomfortable. Even if you're saying, "You look great," you can't help but also send the message that "You didn't look great before." Basically, it's a no-win.

All I really want is to be comfortable in my own skin (which I know will be a lifelong struggle) and for other people to feel that way, too. I'm hoping that I will write this chapter and you will read it and we'll all realize how silly it is that women are so hard on themselves and each other. (Though, having been witness to so much of Chris's press tour for *Guardians of the Galaxy* and even *Zero Dark Thirty*, where the big story was about his weight loss, I learned—again—that this narrative isn't entirely unique to one gender.)

Despite this list of body gripes, I have developed a willingness to be viewed as unattractive, at least in my work, that I certainly didn't have growing up. *Scary Movie* schooled me in letting go of vanity. Not to say I'm not vain, because I'm totally vain, but when I'm doing character work, I feel like it would be a disservice to the women I play to get too wrapped up in the aesthetics.

And should the day come when I'm completely enlightened and have made total peace with my body, I'll still probably be hung up on . . .

## #4. MY HANDS.

I hate my hands.

When Chris Evans and I first worked together on *What's Your Number?,* one day out of nowhere he said to me, "I love your hands."

"Please don't look at my hands," I said, pulling them behind my back.

"No, they remind me of Maggie Somethingorother from the third grade," he said.

Chris Evans is a gem.

The reality is that I bite my nails and have giant knuckles and they're basically German-immigrant potato-farming hands. The only benefit of my hands is that they're small. And they make penises look big.

# List to Live By:
# Sex on the Beach and Thirteen
# Other Things That Sound Better
# Than They Are

1. **Getting a book deal:** It sounds like an amazing and
   wonderful adventure, but actually, it's terrifying. I
   know, poor little actress girl, getting the chance that
   plenty of more talented writers have strived toward
   for decades. But to that end, this exercise feels
   presumptuous. I'm halfway through and I still have
   about one hundred pages left to fill with . . . what? I
   hope you're looking forward to the next seven
   chapters: a dramatic retelling of *The Real Housewives
   of Beverly Hills*. As an actress, the best perk of my job
   is the day I land the gig. It's the thrill of the chase.
   I'm high on the rush of the win, realizing that
   somebody believes in me. Then I wake up the next
   day and realize I actually have to do the job. I have to
   memorize lines and perform and deal with the

pressure I put on myself and make a 6:00 A.M. call time and hold my face for the camera in a way that looks somewhat normal, which has always been a struggle for me. That's what writing this book feels like. Getting the deal was thrilling, assuming I can actually do it well feels cocky.

2. **Gazpacho.** It's soup that is cold.
3. **Hot buttered rum.** I love heat. I love butter. I love rum. Why, oh why, can't it taste as delicious as it sounds?
4. **Backpacking around Europe.** I actually backpacked around Australia in my early twenties so I *am* qualified to say that *that* sucks, and I imagine Europe would be similar.
5. **Driving across the country in an RV.** Anyone who has made this mistake knows it's horrible. I did it when I was wrapping *What's Your Number?* and was in Boston with my three pugs. I'd flown them to Boston, but that was late April, when they could still fly comfortably in the cargo. During summertime, short-nosed breeds can't fly underneath the plane because it's too hot. Now, dear reader, how does a person get her three dogs back to Los Angeles at the end of August when it is unsafe to fly short-nosed breeds? You rent the biggest RV you can find with your new assistant, who also has a dog and a dying cat and wants to relocate to Southern California to start her music career because the whole adventure is

going to be SO FUN!! You're going to stop at all the sites! Even Mount Rushmore! Sure, some days may be long, and sure, you've never even driven a pickup truck, much less a thirty-foot recreational vehicle, but you know what? You were just given that leather-bound journal by that producer who was nice to your face once, so let's put pen to paper and record the tough times, too! We crashed the RV twice on day one. Not to sound too dramatic (fine, I want to), but I truly don't know how we lived. Maybe we didn't and I'm in a weird hell where you have to write down your thoughts and pray that people like them. Hmmm. So after days filled with Big Macs (don't forget to check the height limit at the drive-through!), being terrified of peeing (or anything else) because you don't know how to empty the waste, and sleeping in Walmart parking lots, it's an experience I would shy away from doing again. And I recommend you do the same. Also, sad to say, the cat died.

6. **Sex on the beach.** Unless it's the drink. Though I don't even know what that drink is, so maybe that sounds better than it is, too.

7. **. . . . Or in a hot tub.**

8. **. . . . Or in a car.** Not because wanting someone so badly that you need to take each other right there in your Honda isn't sexy, but if you're having sex with your high school boyfriend in the parking lot of Yost

Park, the cops could come and catch you in the act, bang on your window, and tell you to get home, now. For example.

9. **Meeting strangers at a gas station.** I recently stayed at the Holiday Inn Express in Davis, California, where the deluxe room apparently means two twin beds. I was visiting my brother and his beautifully pregnant wife. I didn't want to sleep on their couch, and I knew I had to work on this book, so I booked a room at the inn. (Well, Mindy, our life-changing assistant, booked it. You know what should go on the list of things that are as good as they sound? Having an assistant.) I couldn't sleep, so I walked across the street to the Exxon station for some Doritos and a bottle of water. And sure enough, there were a couple of gals sitting outside the store with a cardboard sign: TRYING TO GET TO BERKELEY. Perfect! I sat down with them and introduced myself.

The exchange went something like this: "Hi! I'm Anna! Mind if I sit with you guys for a minute?"

"Uhhh, okay."

"Where you going?"

"Berkeley. Like the sign says."

"That's awesome! Why?"

"Our friend died."

"Oh man, I'm really sorry."

Of course I wanted to know how she died, but we were just getting to know each other. They mentioned they'd been sleeping in their car but, between you and me, I didn't see any cars but the ones filling up. I asked them to tell me their stories— of why they were there and where they came from. They were vague and hesitant and looked at me with those eyes that said, "Are you a nutcase?" Or maybe they said, "Are you that girl from *Scream*?" Or "Can you please just give us a few bucks and leave us the fuck alone?" So I did. I gave them $60 and told them I was going back to the Holiday Inn, at which point it was all I could do not to invite them back with me (after all, I did have two large twin beds). I resisted, because I have a family and computers and Ambien. But a few years ago I would have totally invited them to my hotel room. I probably would have tagged along for the funeral, too. I would have given an obnoxious eulogy and created a gulf between these two nice gals and their friends because they brought some nut who paid for gas but clearly needed a lot of attention. But I would have come back with great stories boasting of my own spontaneity and courage and my new friends with dreadlocks.

10. **Hiking the Pacific Crest Trail.** I don't care what Cheryl Strayed says.

11. **Ménage à trois.** Or so I assume.

12. **Waterbeds.**

13. **Game night.** It gets competitive and people get angry, especially at me. Also, I suck at Pictionary.

14. **Couples massage.** Chris and I did a couples massage once in Hawaii. It was the kind on the beach, where you're in a cabana getting rubbed down while people are walking by and it was ridiculous. Was that supposed to be romantic? Were we supposed to hold hands? Chris had a female masseuse and I had a young man who I'm pretty sure had a boner and was pressing it into my forearm. This is not a humblebrag. My husband was right there and all I could think was, *What's happening? What's going on?* while Chris was reaching for my hand. Was I really going to hold hands with my husband while this guy's boner was pressed into me? You'll be shocked to hear we never did it again.

# Listener List:
# Things That Sound Better
# Than They Are, Part 2

I asked folks on Facebook for more suggestions of "things that sound better than they are," and the responses were even more spot-on than I could have imagined.

Here's part two, the listener edition.

1. Picnics
2. Kissing in the rain
3. Las Vegas
4. Turkish delight
5. Being home for the holidays
6. Shower sex
7. A backyard garden
8. Whatever product they are promoting on infomercials
9. Your twenty-first birthday
10. Potlucks
11. An adult costume party

12. Taking the high road
13. Girls' night out
14. Ouija boards
15. Oysters
16. Karaoke
17. High school reunions
18. Camping
19. Escargot
20. Day drinking
21. New Year's Eve
22. Groupon
23. Caviar
24. Riding on the back of a motorcycle

# What's Your Number?
## (And Why Do We Reveal It?)

I've slept with five people, and, at this point, dear reader, you've met them all. Chad, the one-night stand from my college dorm, Dave, Ben, and Chris. My number is five.

*What's Your Number?* came out in 2011. For those of you who missed it (and I think that was a lot of you) I played Ally Darling, a single thirtysomething who reads a magazine article saying that women who sleep with twenty or more guys are unlikely to find a husband. Conveniently, she's had sex with exactly that many men. So she tries to track them down, hoping that "the one" is in that bunch. I was an executive producer on the movie and I loved so much about it, but it didn't resonate with people in the way that I hoped it would. Part of the reason for that, I think, is that sleeping with twenty people doesn't feel like a source of shame these days, and it shouldn't. Looking back, I think the movie's premise in and of itself felt a little bit like, *Who cares how many people we've slept with, and why are we still talking about this? And if we are indeed ashamed of our number, why?* The movie showed a woman who was embarrassed by her sexual history and worried it meant she couldn't be in a stable relationship, but it never really addressed the question of why she felt that embarrassment to begin with. That's the part I wish we had dug into a little more.

I strongly believe that women shouldn't feel any obligation to reveal how many people they've slept with. But if they choose to, they shouldn't be shamed if their list is long, and shouldn't be revered if it's short. And yet, I'm embarrassed to admit that I'm totally guilty of sharing my number as some sort of proof of my own value. Early on in my relationship with Chris, I felt the need to tell him that I'd slept with only four other men. I have no idea why I thought it necessary to share this. It ran counter to all my instincts as a woman who should have felt like she could sleep with however many people she wanted to. I fell into this trap of, *Oh, look, I'm precious! My vagina has barely even been touched!* I hate that I felt that way.

The conversation with Chris took place five or six days after we started dating. He certainly didn't ask me how many guys I'd been with, but I really wanted to tell him, probably because we'd slept together fairly soon after the split from Ben, and getting into bed with someone that quickly was unusual for me. I felt compelled to explain that I didn't normally do this. So I pretty much just blurted it out, completely unprompted. "I've slept with only four other guys!" Even as the words were coming out of my mouth I was thinking, *Why am I saying this? I'm a thirty-year-old adult. What am I trying to prove?* Why was I talking about my number like I was a thoroughbred horse that hadn't run many races? I was so annoyed at myself. But just as Chris Evans in *What's Your Number?* called out my character and said he didn't care about her number, my Chris did the same thing. He was gentle, but he definitely didn't want to know. "I'm not quite sure why you're telling me this," he said.

I was telling him because I thought it would be attractive to him—and that's fucked-up. You know what's not attractive to guys? Thinking about the women they love with other dudes and discussing all the partners they've had. (At least, not usually. Some guys have creepy fetishes, and I can't speak for them.)

Chris told me that whatever I'd done and whomever I'd done it with, it didn't bother him and he didn't need to know.

That, in turn, made me feel pretty embarrassed. I had been not-so-subtly searching for how many women he'd been with, and I'm confident it was a lot more than four or five. He was casual and cool about it when I finally tried to get it out of him. "I don't know," he kept saying. "I really don't know." It was so frustrating. *What do you mean you don't know?* His approach to his sexuality was the opposite of how I viewed my own, which apparently was strictly a numbers game. If it got too high, I thought, somebody somewhere is not going to value me.

This is why I'm terrified at the idea of having a daughter one day. I would love it, but I would also have a lot of complicated feelings regarding teaching her how to view her body and her self-worth. I wouldn't want her to learn any of these crazy "my value is tied to my number" lessons from me. And I say that because I do think my own views in that regard, at least back when I started dating Chris, came largely from my mom. Or maybe it was 80 percent my mom, 20 percent graduating high school in 1994, when there was still very much a stigma of being a slut if you fucked some dude at a keg party.

(Raising a boy comes with its own challenges. It's so important to me that Jack always treats his lovers, or significant others, with respect. I would be furious with him if I heard about a drunken party and got a phone call from some girl's parents saying that Jack took advantage of their daughter last night. There is going to be a day where I need to explain to him that he will have all these crazy urges and he needs to fight them with every ounce of his body. I want to raise a smart, kind son who is strong enough to resist what I imagine will be superintense physical longings. Otherwise he is going to a boarding school in Idaho where they'll beat his ass.)

Looking back now, I wish I *had* slept with more people, simply so I could learn to be a better lover and know how to tackle more positions and make better noises. I am not envious of the people I know who have slept with only three people, but my friend who can't even count the people she's slept with? I'm envious of that. That's a study abroad program that I just never went on. But I don't think I could fundamentally change the part of me that has sex with a lot of emotional investment. If I were to have slept with forty men, the mental exhaustion of it would have wrecked me.

Also, as I found out the hard way, I am a terrible one-night stand. I was really hard on myself the next day, wondering if I made a mistake and if the guy liked me and if I was good in bed and then getting mad at myself . . . doing that more often would have been a disaster. Any degree of empowerment that accompanied my sexual freedom would have been squandered by my need to please even the most random lover. Thus is the curse of the self-obsessed narcissist.

# Comedy, Fame,
# and the Gross Words

**M**y first taste of fame was when I was nineteen. I was walking across the University of Washington campus and this girl came up to me and excitedly said, "I just got hired at Red Robin and you're in the training video!" It was true. I played the perfect hostess who picks up the restaurant phone, looks into the camera, and says: "Here at Red Robin, we *always* give good phone."

Five years ago, Chris and I went to Red Robin and an employee came up to our table. "Oh my God!" she said. "They are still using that training video!"

All I could think was, *Fuck no.*

**I** never expected to end up in comedy. My family maintains that I was a funny kid, but I remember myself, at least in public, as quiet and serious. Funny thoughts were always in the back of my head, but I never said them out loud because it was way too terrifying. I always wanted to be daring, but I couldn't stand the thought of ridicule from my classmates. There was nothing scarier to me than the idea of other kids making fun of me, so I was never the class clown. I was never outspoken. I suppressed a lot. As a result, ending up in comedy was a huge surprise, and I'm still not sure if I've embraced it as my thing. It has not been a Cinderella shoe situation for me at all. So many of the funny people I work with spent their lives trying to succeed in comedy. They were doing standup before they got their big breaks, and before that they were goofing off in front of the class. They had a natural affinity for making people laugh that I never had.

There was one time, when I was working as a receptionist at my father's ad agency, that I remember suddenly understanding the power of landing a laugh. It was the summer before my sophomore year of college and I was filling in for an employee on maternity leave. I felt so important, walking around downtown Seattle during my lunch hour in my little "corporate" dresses. Nothing sexy, just Old Navy stuff. But I'd sit and eat my lunch alongside executives outside in Pioneer Square and I had this feeling like I belonged there. *This is my new world, the corporate world of Seattle.* I would get looks from men and it always felt good, even though I told myself I hated it.

One day, I had a knit dress and my backpack on and I was getting more looks than I normally did, and I started to feel that rage bubble up in me. *This is offensive! Men are pigs!* Of course I also liked attention, otherwise I wouldn't have bleached my hair blond, but that is the constant struggle of being a woman—do we love the leering looks or do we hate them? But I was really starting to brew with anger, until finally this woman in a truck yelled out to me. "Hey, lady! Your ass is showing!" I felt behind me and my dress had creeped up below my backpack and I was wearing granny panties and it was mortifying.

There's nothing like feeling like you have the upper hand and then having your arrogance knocked down ten pegs. It happens to celebrities a lot. You think somebody is recognizing you but really there's something in your teeth. But in that dress mishap moment, all I could do was go back to the office and tell everyone what happened. It felt like the only way to conquer the embarrassment was to vomit the story back up. My co-workers couldn't stop laughing, and that was the first time I thought to embrace the comedy approach. It seemed like a much better strategy than just bottling everything up, because at least making people laugh made me feel powerful. Certainly it was more empowering than feeling shame-faced all day.

My first true experience with comedy acting was playing Cindy Campbell in *Scary Movie*. When I auditioned for the role, I had no idea what I was doing. I just knew that it was my first big Hollywood audition and I wanted the part. I didn't know this at the time, but acting in a spoof movie requires a weird skill set, because it calls for a degree of earnestness, and if nothing else, I was incredibly earnest back then. Even today, sarcasm is something that is fairly unfamiliar to me. It's not my go-to and it certainly wasn't when I was twenty-two and totally new in LA. So when I auditioned, I was totally committed. I never broke character, and Keenen Ivory Wayans, who directed the movie, couldn't stop laughing. Like, really laughing. I was so baffled. What was I doing that was funny? I had no clue. Later into the filming process, in a total moment of "Daddy, please like me," I indulgently asked Keenen why he hired me. "Because you had no idea what you were doing," he told me.

Though I'd acted before *Scary Movie*, landing that role felt like going straight from a high school baseball team to the majors. (Not that I know anything about baseball.) And

*"Scream If You Know What I Did Last Halloween" was the original title for* Scary Movie.

Keenen was right. I really didn't know what I was doing, but I was willing to completely buy into the idea of Cindy Campbell, and the movie was great training in terms of technicality. You had to learn how to bring a banana into frame at exactly the right moment or how to get hit in the head with a microphone or how to rip your shirt open to show your pig nipples. And as absurd as it sounds, that stuff is hard. The physicality of comedy acting—learning how to fall, for example—is taxing.

And so, even though I'd never expected to work in comedy, I was grateful for that education as an actor. Also, I'd never worked that hard in my life. I went from being a lazy college stoner to working fifteen-hour days where things were actually expected of me. That was a great wake-up call. When I got the *Scary Movie* job I truly thought I was already a superhard worker, but it turned out I had no idea what hard work was until that film. It was the kind of work for which you give up everything in your life—your loved ones, your home—to move on location, work long hours, and live out of a hotel. I was doing something I loved and I was really grateful for the role, and I don't mean to sound whiny because I know how fortunate I am, but it was definitely a rude awakening in terms of what a career in acting was going to mean. After filming that part, I started to get the hang of the job and I realized that I'm incredibly privileged, but the tradeoff was prioritizing my career above everything else, and knowing that I'd be working all hours, and always on call, and that came as a bit of a surprise.

The other surprise, I think, was just how successful *Scary Movie* and the franchise became. After the first movie was a success and then the sequel was a hit, I very arrogantly got resentful of the series because I couldn't get auditions for dramatic roles and I had always thought of myself as a really dramatic person. It took me a little while to embrace the idea of playing a stupid character. For a long time I took it personally. I worried that if I'm playing the stupid person, that must mean people thought I was stupid. Once, on social media, someone wrote, "Anna Faris is good in the Scary Movies, but I think it's because she's as dumb as she plays." (You can get one hundred compliments but it's the one nasty comment that wakes you up in the middle of the night.) That type of shit used to really irk me, but now I love that I got my start in a spoof comedy. At this point I wouldn't change a thing about having played Cindy Campbell or about my comedy career. I love the joy that my roles have brought me. Like playing Samantha James in *Just Friends*, which might be the most fun I've ever had playing a character. Our brilliant director Roger Kumble had this vision of Samantha as totally psychotic, and some of my best lines were Roger's in the moment. He'd say, "Yell out, 'Stupid dick!'" and we'd just giggle and continue to push the insanity. One of the craziest scenes was when Samantha eats the toothpaste. On the day we filmed it, Roger suggested it at the last minute and I was just like, "Sure! I love that!" But because it was last-minute, the props department was not prepared for it. If they had been, hopefully they would have given me toothpaste substitute. Instead, I shoved a whole tube of toothpaste in my mouth, and after that I didn't have taste buds for three days. For real. I'd eat a whole bag of spicy Doritos and not taste a thing. With roles like that, I learned to laugh at myself in ways I never could before.

I love the challenge of comedy, too, because it really is unbelievably challenging. Part of the difficulty is surrendering to the lack of vanity—I have to understand that the world is going to view me as a bimbo and make peace with that. And there's been a lot of reward in embracing the flawed characters that I play. But I *was* naive when I came to Hollywood, simply in the sense that I didn't understand how divided this town was, in terms of being a comedic actor or a dramatic actor. They truly are two different worlds.

**S***cary Movie* was released in 2000, and after that I started getting recognized every now and then. I've never smoked crack, but it felt like what I imagine the first hit must be like. An immediate head rush. The first time I felt that very specific kind of ego-driven high was at the movie's premiere in New York. It was my first premiere, and I really felt like I was in this magical ecstasy dream. There were people calling my name—well, they were saying *Anna*, rhymes with *banana*, but I didn't give a shit. Someone lent me a dress and I was staying at a fancy hotel and executives were saying the movie was going to make more than they ever thought possible, and it was an unbelievable, out-of-body euphoria.

After the movie came out I returned to blond (Cindy Campbell was a brunette), so I didn't get noticed in public very often. A couple of times people thought I was Britney Spears, which was flattering. But even though I wasn't consistently being "spotted," I'll admit I had a few ugly celebrity moments.

The worst of it came over Christmas 2002, when I was twenty-six. I went with my brother and cousins to a bowling alley near my parents' place in Washington and, after a couple of hours hanging out at the bar, the manager cut me off. I'd only had two beers and wasn't especially drunk, and I got annoyed, which I think was fair, except that it provoked me to utter that very hideous phrase: "Don't you know who I am?"

As soon as the words came out of my mouth, all I could think was, *What the fuck did I just say?*

The manager's response: "You're out of here." She didn't know, or care, who I was, and I can't say I blame her.

I felt such shame—not for getting kicked out of the bowling alley bar but for uttering those words. Had I really become that gross? Was I really the person who was drunk on her own ego? And what had I done, really? *The Hot Chick*?

When I woke up the next day, I was horribly embarrassed. I could hardly recognize myself. What kind of self-important person utters that phrase? I'm just so glad that we didn't yet live in a world where everyone had their iPhone in hand at all times. There was no social media or viral videos. In that regard, I got lucky. But I didn't know, in that moment, to be thankful that Facebook didn't exist yet. Instead, I kept thinking of how disappointed and mortified my parents would have been if they had heard me say that kind of thing. That knowledge haunted me, and I was ashamed.

Looking back on that evening, at the risk of sounding like a total cliché, I think I was destined to learn that lesson the hard way. In the wake of *Scary Movie*'s early success, it was really difficult to go from merely dreaming of acting in Hollywood to getting a role to suddenly having people kissing my ass who only three days earlier viewed me with skepticism. And of course I wanted to believe that I was as great as everyone was saying I was. It became a mind fuck, and sifting through the noise to find the people I could trust to actually look at my work and see my potential, but also keep me grounded, was tricky.

That night at the bowling alley was a wake-up call. Fifteen years later, I still have complicated feelings about fame. Don't get me wrong—I feel incredibly lucky and grateful to have the life and career that I do. I remember watching Gwyneth Paltrow on *Oprah* after she won Best Actress for *Shakespeare in Love* in the late nineties. Oprah said something like, "You're hugely famous now. What's that like?" Gwyneth described it as "white-hot" and started to complain a little bit. I wasn't famous at all at that point, but I remember seeing that clip and thinking that if I ever succeeded in Hollywood I would never complain about fame like that. But it does make you feel vulnerable; I realize that now.

Truth be told, I have a lot of guilt wrapped up in my success. I'm glad that I feel good about what I do creatively, and I've worked incredibly hard for my career, but there is a degree of embarrassment around getting put on a weird pedestal, and being in a job that's valued more than somebody who does something else for a living that is perhaps more important but not nearly as luxurious.

There's nowhere where Hollywood's self-important attitude is on display more than at awards shows. My brother once told me that no industry in the world congratulates itself as much as the entertainment industry, and he was right. Not that I'm drowning in statuettes, but I should point out that you are holding in your hands a book written by none other than the *High Times* 2007 Stonette of the Year.

The red carpet, for all its fanfare, is actually a really humbling experience. Even if you're at, say, the Oscars, and some people are yelling your name, you end up behind Brad and Angelina or Nicole Kidman and Keith Urban and it's

just . . . well, let's just say you don't have any delusion about who the crowd is there for. Suddenly, what you think is going to be an ego-charged evening becomes sort of humiliating and, if you have any self-awareness at all, you can't stop thinking about what a fucking jerk you are, because who are you trying to fool?

What I'm saying is that I can't take it all too seriously. Especially as people are snapping my photo, it's hard for me not to think, *Can't you see my flaws? I don't deserve this.* I think that's why I always look the slightest bit awkward in red-carpet photos. I don't know how to hold my face, and I always have my mouth just slightly open. You're supposed to pose your leg or hold your jaw in a certain way, but I can't bring myself to do it. It feels so not me. I'm the one blowing a kiss to photographers, which drives my publicist crazy. It's a silly move, and my publicist, God bless her, just wants me to be perceived as a serious actress. But even if I attempted to be calculated and glamorous and look like a Hollywood untouchable on the red carpet, someone would catch me picking my nose, so why even pretend? (Can you imagine a photo of Angelina digging for a booger at the Oscars? No. That's why she really is an untouchable, and I'm me.) There's a perception that if you take yourself seriously on the red carpet, then the industry in general will take you more seriously. Well, except Jennifer Lawrence. She, to her credit, doesn't take herself seriously, and is still considered the pinnacle of a serious actress. But she wasn't in *Scary Movie 1, 2, 3*, and *4*, and she's the face of Dior. I had a Jergens self-tanning campaign once.

Not that it's a competition. Well, I guess the awards are by their very nature a competition, but that's not something I have to worry about just yet. I feel like a virgin in the best way. The worst thing, I think, would be to get nominated for an award, lose, and never get nominated again. You have all these people talking to you every day for two months about your nomination, and then you have to get in a dress and plaster your face and take a Valium and wait to have your name not called. I'm okay with having sidestepped that.

But if I *do* ever get nominated, the good news is that I've delivered plenty of drunken acceptance speeches at Allison Janney's house, where her seven Emmys are perfect for my practice runs. You know, just in case.

# Unqualified Advice:
# The Bush Is Back

The other night I had a dream that I had a huge hairy bush and I lived in a cabin in the mountains. I was nervous, I think, about my huge bush, but I loved being in that cabin.

It's funny that I would have that dream, actually, because I recently started laser hair removal. The place I go to for facials offers the service, and when I was checking out one day they told me they were offering laser service for a discount, so I started doing my bikini area. Why not? I was totally late to the game, though. I was thirty-nine when I started this process that you should probably be starting when you're, like, twenty-five, if you're going to do it. The good news, for those of you considering it: laser is so much less painful than waxing. It hurts, but they have this whole new cooling thing that they use while you're getting the treatment, and it's nothing compared to getting your skin ripped off with hot wax.

To be clear, I'm not bare. I just wanted to get cleaned up so that I wouldn't have to worry about shaving when I put on a bathing suit. After I started, I went to my gynecologist and I was like, "Guess what?! I got lasered! Aren't you proud of me?"

She just looked at me said: "Oh, honey, you're getting lasered *now*? The bush is back!"

This is a Beverly Hills gynecologist. She knows what she's talking about.

It's so like me to do something just as the trend is waning.

Body hair is a complicated issue. Growing up in Seattle, I was incredibly lazy about shaving my legs and was really unknowledgeable about body grooming in general. It wasn't something my mother was especially concerned with, so she didn't teach me much in the way of hair maintenance. I had never been waxed before I moved to LA, and even then I lived here for eight or nine years before I tried it for the first time. I always shaved my bikini line—it wasn't all just free-flowing—but I'd never waxed, and I certainly didn't know that they also did your butt. That was a real surprise.

One time I was at a pool party with a guy I was seeing, and I was wearing a white bikini. As I started walking toward the house from the pool, my date yelled, "Hey, Anna! Your pussy's showing!" I looked down and I was covered, but I think maybe you could see a hint of darkness through the suit? I was so mortified. And I remember everyone looking at me—not at my crotch, but just watching, wondering how I was going to react. I walked away, but it was cruel and humiliating and felt like a truly low blow.

There's a whole thing about body hair when you're pregnant, too. So many people are examining your vagina on a regular basis, and while I was pregnant with Jack I really wanted to know what the protocol was. Are you expected to be more maintained? Is that, like, a courtesy you should be showing your doctor? Or is pregnancy when you are supposed to really embrace your natural motherliness?

Generally, I like to keep myself groomed. But I did grow out my armpit hair once. I was filming *The Dictator* and I played a Williamsburg militant type and when I was cast they asked me if I'd mind not shaving for a while, so I said sure. By three weeks in, it was really starting to get thick. I guess I thought there would be less than there was, but it was a lot and it was kind of straight and wiry but then got curly at the end in this wispy disgusting way. I think I could have handled it better if it was curly from the onset, like a man's beard, but my hair couldn't make up its mind. And it was dark. My pubic hair is not blond but it's not super dark, but my armpit hair was black.

For the duration of filming, that hair became my identity. I couldn't stop thinking about it. Plus, we were filming in New York in the summer, so it was hot and sweaty and just generally unpleasant. As the movie progressed, there would be moments when I was supposed to raise my arms, and even while we were shooting I could see the look in the crews' eyes when they spotted my pits. There was horror in those eyes.

The hairy armpits definitely affected my feelings of attractiveness. I wish I could have been like, "I am woman! I own this shit." But I just couldn't. I did not own that shit.

I do remember the very real struggle of trying to hail a cab in New York during that time. I'd keep my elbows glued to my rib cage in the least aggressive taxi hail ever. The hair was kind of like a giant tattoo. When something on your body goes against the norm in that way, it becomes a badge, whether you like it or not. You have to understand that it will be a talking point behind your back. And for some people that is what they want, but I just can't handle the inner demons of that. I'm an actress. I care too much what other people think.

Chris was in LA while I shot *The Dictator*, and I can't imagine he loved the hairy pits, but if he hated them, he never let on. He was just like, "Babe, you've got this." One of the great things about being married to an actor is that he really admires the ownership of a role. So we would talk late at night about the decision of a certain line or creating my character and all that nerdy-actory stuff, and he'd tell me he was turned on by my dedication. "It's thicker than my armpit hair, but the way you own that role is sexy," he'd say. A lie, but such a sweet, sweet lie.

Still, all I could think was, *When can I shave this off?* The night we wrapped, I got home late, like at 5:00 A.M., and before I even got in bed I went in the shower and shaved. It was so satisfying to watch as my hair clogged up the drain.

A couple of hours later I got a call asking if I could hold off shaving, in case we had reshoots.

Thank God for armpit doubles.

# Can I Marry You?

I am an ordained minister.

You know how some people get ordained online because they've been invited to officiate the wedding of close couple friends? So they stand up in front of the crowd and tell stories about the bride and groom and speak about love and devotion and the beauty of building a life together? And then after the ceremony is over all the guests congratulate the officiant and want to shake his or her hand because oh my God their words were so personal and touching and they brought tears to everyone's eyes and why don't they just quit their day job because this was certainly their calling and they were so much better than a real minister could have ever been?

None of that has happened to me.

I got ordained out of boredom.

If you haven't already picked up on this, I do a lot of weird shit for no other reason than to entertain myself.

For example, you know those stickers on the back of trucks that read "Problem with my driving? Call 555-5555"? Every now and then when I'm on the road I'll call and just say, "Truck 313131 is a wonderful driver." A real, live person always answers the phone—always a woman—and they are completely shocked to hear from me. Then they say, totally confused, "Ummm, I've never heard this before. So good to know. Uh, thank you." And I'm like, "Yup! They are obeying all the traffic laws!" I take total delight in the operator being completely shocked that someone is calling to report something positive. I just get a real kick out of myself.

When I was in Phoenix filming *Take Me Home Tonight*, I was hanging out, kind of bored, in my temporary apartment one night. What better time to become a minister with the Universal Life Church? It seemed like a good credential to have on my résumé, and maybe one day a couple would ask me to marry them. I fantasize about having the power to do something like that. Also, I wanted bragging rights. I wanted to announce to people that yup, I'm a minister, I can marry you right now! Ask me for advice, too. A minister!

All you have to do is agree that you will attempt to be a good person and you're in. Universal Life Church. Easy peasy.

You can also pay $50 or $60 to get the framed certificate, which Chris did once we started dating. I registered under Anna "White Unicorn" Faris, and my documentation sits right next to my 2007 *High Times* Stonette of the Year Stony Award for *Smiley Face*. The award is a giant bong. It's the only award I've ever won, but I'm beyond thrilled about it. If I die—or, when I die, I guess—I don't want to *only* be remembered for that award, but it should probably be a big part of my legacy. In the entertainment world, where we give each other awards for the most ridiculous shit, I am proud to have the Stony. It's pretty fucking cool.

Back to White Unicorn. You're probably thinking, *But you hate weddings!* True, but I don't hate them across the board, I just hate the bad elements that weddings bring out in people. I hate the frenzy and the drama, and I hate that sometimes the focus gets taken away from where it belongs.

But to officiate a wedding? That's different. I love the idea of bestowing such a grand gesture upon people. Now, that's power.

I got ordained in 2007, and still have yet to minister a wedding. I signed up for my certification with the blind hope that one day I'd get asked, but . . . still waiting on those requests.

A decade later my minister credentials still hold up. There might be state-by-state rigmarole—like I might have to fill out some paperwork if I'm going to marry someone in Mississippi—but that's cool. A small price to pay to get the power vested in me.

# Unqualified Advice:
# Unicorns Aren't Found,
# They're Made

**D**uring the decade or so that Chris and I were together, social media took on a life of its own. We were married in 2009, and Instagram, for example, hadn't launched until 2010, so we certainly didn't have any strategy when we began sharing moments from our personal lives in these public forums. But when Chris started his Instagram feed—posting pictures of the braid he did in my hair or of Jack and me on a porch swing—it was flattering that people responded so positively. It was a huge compliment that folks really seemed to admire, or at least get a kick out of, the two of us as a couple.

It's hard to know why people reacted that way—what did they see that made Chris and me stand out for them?

I like to think that fans picked up on the fact that we really enjoyed each other's company. There are loads of pictures out there where I'm guffawing at something Chris is saying on the red carpet—usually it was something about our mutual feelings of "What are we doing here? We're just two kids from Washington! Did they get this right?" We both have a bit of impostor syndrome when it comes to red carpet events. We're not glamorous Hollywood, or at least we don't feel that way; so we definitely shared a sentiment of "Are they going to figure out we don't belong here?"

There's also the fact that we both come from comedy. I think people relate to comedy actors a little more, overall.

I had a hard time adjusting to social media, to be honest. I didn't come up in the Hollywood world where you publicize your every move. I was taught that you hide from paparazzi and you don't talk about your relationships or personal stuff; you talk only about the movie or the project. But as we delved deeper into the world of social media, we unknowingly cultivated an image of the perfect Hollywood couple—perfect, I guess, in a down-to-earth, just-regular-people kind of way. And mostly it was lovely—we *were* happy and in love, and we really *are* just regular goofballs, so it felt fairly easy to keep up the idea of #relationshipgoals.

A while back, Chris asked me if I felt a lot of pressure from being in a high-profile relationship, and I told him that I did—it was an odd circumstance. That he was asking the question made me think that he probably felt that way, too. No one wants to live their lives according to a hashtag. Still, it felt that a good offense was the best defense. So instead of being a couple who never spoke publicly about their relationship, we posted silly photos. We tried to let people into our lives to some degree, and that became a joy for us, because we mostly got positive and loving feedback, and, who are we kidding, that feels really good.

Of course, social media hasn't *always* been kind to us. I've had a few stints of bullying on Twitter—angry fans saying cruel things—and it totally hurts my feelings. Well, a lot of things hurt my feelings, so maybe I'm not a great example, but it would be a very odd person who is completely numb to something really nasty that is said about them. Most actors have built their careers off the idea of being creative but also around questions like, *Are people going to like me? Are they going to like my work?* That's why they cry when they win an Oscar, because it's validation that audiences appreciate them. It's easy to laugh at Sally Field's "You like me!" moment, but I'm sure that's what most winners are thinking. So much of our success relies on appealing to viewers, and I think only a sociopath would be completely numb to the cruelty of strangers' nasty digs.

I imagine that strangers who vocalize their negative opinions about celebrities just want to be heard, but the nastiness confuses me because it would never occur to me to write to Jodie Foster and say, "I didn't like that dress that you wore." The motivation there is baffling to me. That said, I've written one fan letter in my life. In college I wrote to the band 311, and it was a really angry letter. Before they got big on the national scene, they had two albums that my friends and I loved. We went to their concerts and felt like we were true fans who appreciated their art, even if it wasn't mainstream. Then they came out with a single called "My Stony Baby" and I thought it was a new, sellout sound for them. So I wrote

a letter to say how they had disappointed me. I'm sure they appreciated my self-righteous lecture that was literally like, "I can't believe the direction you've turned." I never heard back.

Despite a few bouts of negativity, overall, Chris and I were lucky to have had mostly positive interactions on social media, and we liked Instagram and Twitter because they were great places to communicate the reality that we were just a silly little family.

Or something. I don't know.

I bring all this up because one of the most common questions we have gotten on the podcast from single female listeners is: "How do I find a unicorn like Chris?"

But I think the question is less about how someone can find

a guy just like Chris (though he *is* funny and hot and kind, and those aren't bad things to look for in a partner) and more about how to find a relationship that is fun and respectful and loving and that appears, even to outsiders, like a happy one. And I do have some thoughts on that, unqualified as they may be.

The first is simple: Know what you're looking for. It took a lot of maturing over time on my part to get to a place where I could recognize a kind person, and also to know that that's what I wanted. It took almost the entirety of the time that Chris and I worked together before I realized that I actually wanted a man who is happy and who other people got along with. And that remains true. Being around a content and well-liked person makes for a more pleasant relationship in general. That doesn't mean the partnership will be perfect, or that you don't still have to work at it, but it will be more likely to entail an element of respect that will reverberate through your relationship no matter how it unfolds.

So know what you want.

But also, look around at who's already in your orbit. It's easy, I think, to overlook a lot of the people in our lives because we think we are looking for something entirely new. But don't necessarily write off a good person that you already know. Recognize a good person, and open yourself up to him or her.

I also happen to believe that women listen to their friends' critiques way too much. Sometimes those voices are important, like when a friend recognizes that the guy you're with makes you feel like shit, but the stuff that is not important is the "he's not that hot" or "he works for UPS" or whatever petty put-downs they unload on you. Being able to ignore the unhelpful feedback from friends is hard, but so important.

Guys are guilty of it, too. I talk about this with Sim some-times, the idea that the minute a guy's friends say, "She's a six," or whatever lame things men tell each other about the women they're seeing, the next thing you know, that guy has broken up with a great person for no reason. So I think one of the best skills anyone can have is the ability to cherry-pick the friends who have good intentions and want the best for you, and the friends who just say gnarly stuff like, "He's not rich enough," simply to pass judgment. That takes a ton of matu-rity, though, because those voices land hard. When Chris and I started dating, one of my friends gave me her review: "He's okay," she said, "but he's such a boy." At the time Chris was new in my life and that comment really hurt my feelings.

"I know, I know," I said. "He still throws darts at the wall in his apartment and I don't know how often he changes his sheets. But he's so sweet." I was at a place by then where I could see a much bigger picture than his supposed childish ways. And eventually he made the bed every morning!

But I'll be frank. You can know what you're looking for, open yourself up to folks already in your life, and ignore your friends' catty feedback, and still end up disappointed. Is that too harsh? I don't mean it to be, but I think it's important to be upfront about the fact that these small nuggets of advice aren't the keys to relationship happiness. They can help you find love, maybe, but once you've met someone, you can't turn him into the person you want him to be—the inner tools have to be in him. If those lean toward angry and unhappy or playing the victim, you can't change those things on your own.

When we get the unicorn question, I like to joke that unicorns aren't found, they're made. And while the foundation of a man's makeup can't necessarily be tweaked, there are some behaviors that can be honed over time, if you're smart about your approach. I like to think of it less as changing a man, and more of, let's say, *adjusting* him.

For example: As I've already mentioned, Chris used to be late all the time. With me, with appointments, everything. He had no time-management skills. After that time I left the house because he showed up an hour late when I was cooking, he changed his ways. He's not always perfectly prompt, but he's on time enough that it stopped driving me crazy and wasn't a point of conflict. I take some credit for his newfound semi-punctuality, because I made clear I wasn't just going to wait all the time, but I also think it was a testament to how much he wanted to be in the relationship, because he was willing to change in order to be with me.

A lot of the work in turning your regular man into a unicorn man (a uniman? manicorn?) is simply figuring out the best way to tell them what you want. Take Chris. He loves lists. Loves them! So while it may not always have occurred to him to clean the kitchen, or to put away the suitcase that was sitting in the hallway for a week, when I put it on a list, he would scrub that kitchen like his life depended on it and unpack that suitcase like a pro. He was never grumpy about doing chores at all, he just didn't always think of them. That's where the list came in handy.

Finally, there's a lot of power in the words *thank you*. When Chris does something that I'm grateful for, even if it's small, I thank him, and I know he appreciates that. And he thanks me often, too. Courtesy has always been really important with us. Some couples tease each other a lot, and that's not necessarily bad, but it's a slippery slope. Harmless teasing can quickly lead to hurtful teasing, and public teasing inevitably spirals into a fight on the drive home, and then you're in a really shitty spot.

So there you go. Create a unicorn in three simple steps! Of course, even when you have a unicorn, relationships don't necessarily follow the journey you'd envisioned. But that's always the case; and if you've been lucky enough to catch a unicorn, you can at least count on kindness and respect. And that pretty much counts for everything.

# Chatroulette

**F**or a brief period in late 2009, I played a lot of Chatroulette. It was magical.

Chatroulette, in case you don't remember its brief heyday
as king of the Internet, was (or maybe still is?) a website in
which strangers from across the globe were randomly paired
up to chat, visit new worlds, hear different perspectives, and
basically just connect live. Unfortunately, like so many things,
it got ruined by rampant penises.

In late 2009 and early 2010, I spent a few months in the woods
north of Auckland, New Zealand, shooting *Yogi Bear*. It was a
long shoot, especially because the movie was in 3-D. Shooting
a movie in 3-D is incredibly technical, and so much of the work
was weather dependent. We would start to shoot a scene and a
cloud would come overhead, so we'd have to stop filming, or
we'd have people shaking massive cicada-like creatures out of
the trees because they were so loud. There were some days
where we wouldn't shoot anything at all, so it was just me and
the four or five dudes in the cast, hanging out in the woods.

Most days, I'd eat lunch in my trailer with T. J. Miller, who played one of the park rangers. That's when he introduced me to Chatroulette. My memory is a little hazy on why we had Wi-Fi access yet horrible phone service, but that was indeed the case, so the two of us would log on and talk to people all over the world.

For those of you who never played Chatroulette, here's how it worked: You logged onto the website and a box would pop up that said something like, "Want to play?" Then you'd click yes and get matched with a random person, or group of people, who could be anywhere in the world—a woman in a dark basement in Lithuania or a bunch of wasted dudes in Greece. For the most part, everybody we encountered was shrouded in darkness, perhaps because we were the only people playing on their lunch break. Everyone else seemed to wait until after hours. The darkness was especially striking because we were in RV trailers in the middle of the day with light pouring in through the windows. But however weird it seemed to T.J. and me to encounter a group of guys pounding beers in Pakistan, it was probably exponentially more jarring for them to happen upon a guy in a park ranger outfit in a crazy-bright trailer in the middle of the New Zealand forest.

Eventually I started logging on by myself. This was before Chatroulette became masturbation central, and I loved that I connected with people who had no ties to me, and mostly didn't know who I was. Later on in Chatroulette's existence it became apparent that people could take a screenshot of the person they were talking to, but at this time it was all so new.

You'd get paired up with a random person, and if someone freaked you out or you didn't like them you could just click "next" and instantly go somewhere else in the world, and they could do the same to you. So there was an element of risk— Who were you going to see? Would they like you?—but once you connected with someone you just chatted. The beautiful thing about it, I thought, was that there was no small talk. It was straight to the good stuff: *What are you looking for? Where are you? What do you want out of this? Are you happy?*

I love getting to know strangers instantly, skipping the niceties and getting right to the heart of a discussion. Who wants to talk about the weather? This is California—it's always sunny. There literally hasn't been anything new to say about the weather for years. I'm also an overexplainer, which speaks to my small-talk deficiencies. Instead of engaging in proper chitchat, I tell people too much about myself too early, even when they have zero interest. If I ask a flight attendant for a glass of chardonnay, I immediately get into how I had a crazy night last night. It's not until I see their face, wearing the *mm-hhmm* smile of a person who couldn't care less, that I remember that they don't give a fuck. I do it at work, too. The crew calls me to set and I say, "I'll be right down—I just need to pee and wash my hands and brush my teeth." Why do I do that? They don't need that visual. But it would never occur to me to stop at "I'll be right down."

With Chatroulette, it really was a gift to have random and honest interactions with people who knew nothing about me. I talked to a librarian in Texas for an hour and a half about books and about life and about her depression and loneliness, and shared that I was lonely, too. I was lucky to be visiting this beautiful country, but I was away from the people I loved, so I could relate to her struggle. Then I connected with a gal in Milan who spoke English really well and we talked about boyfriends for a while. And I talked to a lot of really obnoxious girls in the UK. Once I landed on two girls who were doing meth and were pretty open about it and they said, while seemingly strung out, "You need to get a nose job."

"So this is what you guys do?" I asked. "You go on Chatroulette and you're just mean to people?"

They paused for a moment, as if wondering if they should actually talk to this person who was calling them out. Then they whined, "You're annoying us," and nexted me. I do remember it stinging, though, the nose-job thing.

Chatroulette was a crazy and wonderful experiment, where you got to study abroad briefly and got to hear another person's perspective on something without any of the associated risks of being a stranger in a strange land. I loved the purity of that. The Hollywood bubble can be kind of isolating sometimes, which is why I love the escapism of reality TV and books and podcasts. It's why I have a podcast myself, and why that podcast involves asking people to tell me their problems within moments of us meeting over the phone. But in some ways, Chatroulette was an even more authentic outlet for my curiosity and my desire to connect with the world outside of show business.

Looking back on it, I think my experience with Chatroulette was the last time I was able to engage with strangers with absolutely no celebrity bullshit surrounding the interaction. I don't think there's anyone I meet today where the fact that I'm a semi-well-known actress isn't somehow informing the exchange. It doesn't actually matter that I'm an actress, obviously. It's just a job. But fame often changes the way people interact with me.

The magic of Chatroulette was short-lived. The site pretty quickly turned into a sea of men masturbating, which was disappointing. These men were too cowardly to show their faces, of course, so the camera would just land on their dicks.

I was so confused when Chatroulette became a forum for guys to show off their penises. I can't imagine any scenario in which I would enjoy filming a close-up of my vagina or getting off on somebody else looking at it. I just don't understand the arrogance of "look at this swollen member." It takes women until we're like seventy-eight to peer at ourselves down there.

Ultimately, I was pissed that this cool forum where I had gotten to know strangers outside of the celebrity space was being taken away from me. I would hit next repeatedly and it would take seven, then thirty-two, then seventy-four times just to find a non-masturbator. So, what, you're going to spend two hours until you find a view that isn't of a penis? Eventually I decided to take out my anger on these men by cheering for them. I'd put on my best, most high-pitched cheerleader voice and be like, "You can do it! Let's go! Let's go! Rub hard! You can finish! Yay, go, rah-rah!" The idea was to annoy them so much that they'd next me, and eventually—after like two to four minutes—they would, but I was always surprised at how long they would stay on me with my annoying chants. Maybe they were like, "This girl thinks I can do this!" or maybe they were just excited to not land on a penis themselves. I never saw anyone go to completion, though, thank God. The goal was to frustrate them, and I usually succeeded.

Ultimately I stopped using Chatroulette. Because of the dicks, sure, but also because I came home from New Zealand and I wasn't so lonely anymore. I wasn't desperate for someone to talk to, so I could connect in person rather than traveling to a basement in Lithuania. But also, the dicks.

# How to Deal with Jealousy

**N**ewsflash: Jealousy is the worst. It's a normal human emotion that is amplified in a competitive world like Hollywood and amplified even more when you are married to someone in Hollywood who keeps getting roles opposite sexy costars.

People regularly ask me what it feels like to see the person you love kiss somebody else on-screen. And most of the time, it's really not a big deal. It's part of the job and I know that to be true, because I'm in the same business. But I've had my moments. Like when Chris worked with some of the most beautiful and charming women in the world. I'm not *not* human.

I have a strategy to deal with jealousy. If I feel twinges of it, whether it was toward Chris's smokin' hot costars, or actors whose careers are more successful than mine, I try hard to befriend them and compliment and love them. Not in a fake, frenemy way, but for real. Because 95 percent of the time it's hard to have jealous or catty feelings toward someone you really like.

Also, there's no other option. Regardless of whether your boyfriend or husband is a movie star or a teacher, if he works with women, you might find yourself dealing with moments of envy. And, short of forcing him to quit (a strategy I do not endorse), you're going to have to live with that reality. In my case, Chris worked with multiple women who are hot and funny and charming and hugely successful, so what was I going to do? It's unattractive, and unproductive, to be catty, so the only other option was to go on the offensive: "Will you please be my friend?" I've found it to be an effective strategy to avoid driving yourself crazy.

For a long time, I felt really lucky. Even though Chris was becoming hugely famous and I'd been sort of famous for a while, the two of us led such boring lives that the tabloids usually left us alone. The paparazzi will follow you sometimes, but there are specific places you go if you want to be photographed, and Chris and I just weren't there. We were homebodies.

But when Chris filmed *Passengers* with Jennifer Lawrence, that all changed. Even before they met in person, my publicist, out of the blue, pulled me aside. "Anna, listen, there are going to be paparazzi all over them," she said. "There are going to be shots of them laughing together on their way to set. There are going to be stories circulating, and you have to brace yourself for this." I didn't think it would bother me. I've been in this business a while now and I had seen Chris star alongside other beautiful women, like Aubrey Plaza and Bryce Dallas Howard. But then, when it actually started and magazines began running rumors, it was totally hurtful. There was one article where they showed this lonely picture of me walking down the beach alongside photos of Jennifer and Chris on the red carpet and the story was something like, "Chris is enamored of his costar, and his wife, Anna, is sad and feels like an aging actress!" I mean, I do feel like an aging actress, but that has nothing to do with this. (Also, I'm pretty sure that photo was taken on a family beach trip, and Chris and Jack were ten steps behind me.)

I talked to Chris about how hurt I felt, even though I knew there was no truth to the stories, and he didn't understand it at first. "Why are you even paying attention to that?" he asked.

But I wasn't reading the tabloids or seeking the rumors out—people were telling me about them. I didn't want to pay attention to the stories but I couldn't block them all out, either. I'd always taken pride in our relationship, and the coverage, even though it was just false rumors, was making me feel insecure. Eventually Chris came around and understood why it felt shitty. Jennifer and I really are friendly, and she was apologetic even though she didn't need to be, because she hadn't done anything wrong. She's awesome, but of course it's hurtful and also embarrassing when people are saying your husband is cheating on you—even if it's patently untrue. You still feel, and look, like a fool. But that's something I have had to learn to handle in stride. When you're a semi-public figure, married to another public figure, in a very public relationship, you don't really have much choice.

I know Chris has felt the same way in the past, and for that I'm grateful. I think a small amount of jealousy is healthy in a relationship, and a number of my exes were frustratingly not jealous. Not that I ever wanted Chris to feel bad, but I felt like it was okay if he believed I was a desirable person and that there were men who'd love to whisk me away. That wasn't so much an issue while making *Mom*. I barely have any love interests on the show and even when I do, it's such an unsexy format. But when Chris and I first started dating, and then later when I was making *What's Your Number?* Chris had his jealous moments. We filmed that movie in Boston and Chris Evans played my love interest. While my Chris had a break from filming *Parks and Recreation,* he came to set and did a small part. He was never overt about it, but he would bring up my kissing scenes with Chris Evans casually. "So, when do you have to do that love scene with Evans?" he'd ask. It was thinly veiled, but very sweet. That passed within days, though, when he used my own jealousy strategy to his advantage.

I had an early shoot one morning, but my Chris and Chris Evans did not. So they went out on the town the night before, and the next day they were best friends. They couldn't get enough of each other. I was like, "Okay, I get it, nobody's jealous anymore because you guys are best buds. Awesome." They were so enamored of each other that I still ended up being the jealous one clamoring for attention. *Hey, guys! Look at me!*

I've been the romantic interest in movies, too, but—and maybe I'm being naive—I really don't think I've been the cause of much jealousy on the part of the women in my costars' lives. It's a combination of being a woman in comedy and having been married with a kid. I eliminated any possible threat to serious actresses. You're safe with Anna! She's not going to take your man *or* your job!

# Turning the Tables:
# How Would You Proceed?

For the "How Would You Proceed" segment on *Unqualified*, coming up with the just-right scenario for each guest is one of the best parts of episode prep, and listening to people talk their way out of awkward moments—whether it's a bite into the raw chicken that Oprah cooked them for dinner, a surprise moment in bed with Javier Bardem, or a request to be the face of adult diapers in Japan—has been a joy. Cassie and I talked about how I'd proceed in some similarly insane predicaments.

*You just started dating a guy and he nicknames your vagina Marie Antoinette. He only refers to it as Marie Antoinette. How would you proceed?*

**Anna:** I think I would giggle a bit and think it was a little strange but I don't think I would comment on it. Or maybe I'd say, "Let them eat cake!" After a couple of years if I was really into him I'd be like, "So are you really into the French Revolution? Should we go to Versailles?" There are so many things he could say that would be so much worse, but Marie Antoinette would be kind of amusing. I wonder what he would call his penis. I'm fascinated by the idea of naming genitalia and the kinds of people who would do that. It's usually men, I think, so I would definitely want to know if he refers to his penis as something.

*You are dating a guy, Kevin, for three months. You hang out a lot. He travels frequently for work, and has told you that he's a businessman. He's superathletic, handsome, and seems like a really good guy. Suddenly he goes radio silent. He doesn't return any calls or messages. Two weeks later you hear from him and he says, "I'm so sorry. I really wanted to contact you but I couldn't. I have to be honest: I'm a spy and I was on a secret mission protecting our country." How would you proceed?*

 Anna: "Wow, Kevin. Is Kevin your real name?"

Cassie: "It is."

 Anna: "I've got to tell you, I was hurt that I didn't hear from you. I'm confused. Am I supposed to know that you are a spy or is it top secret?"

Cassie: "I can only tell people I trust and care about, and I trust and care about you. I work for the CIA. I can't tell you any more than that. So sometimes I disappear. Is this a relationship you think you can continue with?"

Anna: "I think so. I'd love to maybe discuss this further, though I know you probably can't give me a lot of information. Is everything you've told me about your life and childhood true?"

Cassie: "For the most part, yes."

Anna: "For the most part?"

Cassie: "I've changed some names. But they all know I work for the government."

Anna: "The only thing that worries me, I guess, is that you might be lying. I'm sure you can understand that. You probably have a suspicious mind, too, since you're a spy."

Cassie: "Sure, I could see how it could appear that way."

Anna: "It's not that you're married, right? And have another family?"

Cassie: "No. You just have to trust me."

Anna: "Is your life in danger a lot?"

Cassie: "Not while I'm here in Los Angeles. Maybe when I'm abroad. Look, I hope this doesn't change anything between us."

Anna: "Well, I think it will be hard if we're in a relationship and I'm waiting for you to pick me up and you've disappeared."

Cassie: "I'm supportive of your career, Anna. I'd like it if you were supportive of mine."

Anna: "I love our country, but I feel like we haven't known each other very long. Can you give me a little time? Actually, you know what I've just realized? You met my friend Elizabeth, right? Well, over the last couple of months I think I've fallen in love with her. I think I'm a lesbian. Thank you for protecting our country. Keep fighting the good fight, okay?". . . . I was willing to give Kevin the benefit of the doubt at first. I was hoping the story would add up, but it definitely started to seem like he was lying. Long term, could I date a spy? Maybe. Chris has Navy SEAL buddies from his time filming *Zero Dark Thirty* who would talk about how they got calls in the middle of the night and would have to just leave and they couldn't say what they were doing. They got the call and they were out—and they do the most dangerous stuff and their wives don't know where they are. But Kevin could have just been supercreepy, with a wife and child.

*You are about to have sex for the first time with your guy of the month, a forty-year-old hottie named Todd. Just before you do the deed, he says, "I'm so glad I waited all these years. I'm a virgin. Let's make this special." How would you proceed?*

**Anna:** Have we talked about his previous relationships before?

**Cassie:** Nothing too detailed. He's had serious relationships before, but he wanted to wait for marriage or someone he thought was really the right, special girl.

**Anna:** I think I'd be like, "Let's do it!" I've never had sex with a virgin. I would probably feel like, *Whoa, my vagina is magical.* It would be a huge ego boost. I would want to ask him questions, but if things are getting hot and heavy—I'm thinking more like a dude right now than I usually do, but I think I would have sex now and ask questions later. Selfishly, I'd want to have that experience, though I'd definitely feel the weight of, *Oh boy this is big for this person.* I'd probably say something like, "Are you sure you're ready? I would love to have sex with you but I want to make sure that you feel ready and if you do I'm glad." The sex probably wouldn't be that good or that long, but I'd hope he'd be happy with the sensation. And maybe later on I would ask about the other gals. What happened with them? Were they just okay with waiting? Did they do other things? Oral? Anal? But yeah, I think I would do it.

# Jack Pratt

I got pregnant at thirty-five. Chris and I tried for a year. We did that thing everyone does, where I went off birth control, which I'd been on since I was seventeen, and figured I would get pregnant right away. We didn't know enough about the whole process to realize that that was optimistic, so we approached getting pregnant with a lot of romance. Rather than bothering ourselves with checking my ovulation or taking my temperature or any of that stuff that maybe is actually useful, we just thought we'd burn some candles and set the mood and poof! A baby.

It didn't work exactly like that. Six or seven months passed and I didn't get pregnant. Chris was traveling all the time for work, and while I would say we had a healthy sex life, it wasn't like we were having sex every night—that would just be weird. So we decided that if a year passed and I still wasn't pregnant we'd consult a doctor.

At right around the one-year mark, I started to feel weird. I had to pee all the time. I was bloated and was more tired than usual and so hungry. For whatever reason, the frequency with which I was peeing was the major sign for me. Of course I must have missed my period, but I don't remember getting hung up on that. It was simply, *Why the fuck do I have to pee so much?*

So I took a pregnancy test and it was so thrilling. And then my doctor, whom I adore, called me and was like, "Since you're thirty-five, you're a geriatric pregnancy." *Huh*, I thought. *That's new.* It's such a horrifying term. But despite *geriatric* conjuring the image of a ninety-year-old grandmother with a watermelon under her girdle, I actually had a really lovely pregnancy. I never felt ill. Chris and I were both excited and happy and ready to be Mom and Dad. Jack was growing at a great rate. And I just loved eating. I have a small frame and I hover around 110 pounds, but I was close to 180 by the time I was seven months in.

But, as those of you who've been pregnant know, it can be boring. You can't drink and all you want to do is binge on TV shows and you're tired and your brain generally feels numb. I was filming the British comedy *I Give It a Year* in England and Chris was doing *Zero Dark Thirty* in Jordan, and he'd travel to visit me when he had the chance. After my twenty-week so-nogram I had my British obstetrician put the sex of the baby in an envelope, and when Chris came to visit we sat in a hot tub—well, a lukewarm tub, because when you're pregnant you can't do anything fun—and did the big reveal. It was a really wonderful time.

Soon after that we both finished our movies and went home to LA—Chris to *Parks and Rec* and me to my nesting phase. We got a crib and went to baby CPR class and did all the stuff that first-time parents do.

By the time I was thirty weeks in, I was feeling lucky. Sure, I had restless legs and backaches, but I was active and my regular ultrasounds were all good, and compared to the horror stories I'd heard from some friends, I was having an easy time. Then, on the morning of August 10—when I was thirty weeks and one day—I woke up at two fifteen to a massive gush. The bed was soaked, and even though I felt the fluid coming out of my vagina, I smelled it to make sure it wasn't pee. For those of you who haven't had babies, let me assure you: You can't really mistake your water breaking for peeing. They are entirely different sensations. But when you aren't due for two more months and you're taken by surprise by a sudden burst of fluid, you will pray that it's urine, and you'll go as far as sticking your nose in it if necessary.

I was completely unprepared for anything dramatic like that to happen. I called my OB's office, and I'll never forget the way the on-call doctor said, very calmly, "Sooooo, you need to go to Cedars-Sinai. *Right now.*"

Even after that phone call, it never really occurred to me that Jack was coming. I thought, *I'll go to the hospital, then maybe I'll be home in a few hours.* I know that sounds stupid, it *was* stupid, but I was in denial. My pregnancy had been so drama-free. I thought they'd stitch me up (is that a thing?) and send me on my way, but I certainly didn't think I was in labor. Chris took it more seriously than I did. Serious isn't the right word. It's not that I wasn't serious; I was just in shock. So

Chris threw some underwear and socks in a bag, but he knew enough to know there wasn't time for anything else.

We arrived at the hospital at two forty-five and since this was the middle of the night in Los Angeles, the emergency room was packed. The nurses put me in a wheelchair and rushed me into a room, where they immediately started pumping me full of magnesium, which had a 50 percent chance of stopping labor. It felt horrible. I could sort of feel it going through my veins and it was incredibly painful—the best way I can describe it is like having a headache throughout your entire body. There were a lot of medical professionals in that room, and that's when the fear really set in, as well as the reality that my son might be coming two months early. The magnesium worked, fortunately, but the doctors were very clear that I would not be leaving the hospital until my baby was born.

So they put me on bed rest. A lot of people think bed rest sounds amazing—you can skip work and watch TV and no one can fault you! Living the dream! But the goal was to be on bed rest for four weeks, to give the baby another month to grow. And this was not the kind of easy bed rest where you hang out on the couch but can sneak out to pee or get a snack. This was hospital bed, catheter, no showers, no standing up, ever. I didn't know how to occupy my brain—I was too on edge for books, so I watched movies all day, which sounds fun until you're watching *The Mummy* for the sixth time.

Chris was amazing. He decorated my room with posters and photos and he came to the hospital every night after work with desserts for me and, sometimes, a six-pack of beer for himself, and he'd just sit with me and hold my hand or crawl into my bed. I loved when he brought the beer because he'd get a little buzz, which always made me giggle. He slept there every night.

Days were lonely, but I didn't want any visitors except Chris. The look of concern on people's faces when they saw me really stressed me out. There's nothing worse than being sick and yet feeling like you have to be the one reassuring others, which is exactly how I felt. Also, I was in that bed-gown thing and I was big and puffy and I had really short hair that I was trying to grow out (priorities) and the whole combination just felt like, *Please, please go away.*

In the early morning of my seventh day of bed rest (I made it sound like a year, I know, and it felt that way) I started cramping really badly. You know how on that show *I Didn't Know I Was Pregnant* the women always just thought they had to poop? I get that. Contractions really do feel like you have to take a shit, so that's what I thought this was. Or, at least, that's what I told myself it was, because I was in denial. I tried to downplay the intensity of the pain until around noon, when the nurses finally called it. "No, this is labor," they said.

I tried to convince them otherwise, because I wasn't prepared, but I'd just reached the thirty-one-week marker, which was a big deal. When a baby is that early, even one extra week in the womb goes a long way, and decreases that baby's chances for long-term health concerns.

What followed was, in some respects, a blur. Chris came rushing in. The pain was so crazy that I could barely speak. I do remember asking my ob-gyn, "If he's this early and he's going to be so little, shouldn't it hurt less?" She laughed at me and said, "Oh no, that's not how this works."

I eventually got an epidural, which I appreciated because it made me feel present in the moment, as opposed to the stabbing, piercing back pain that is unlike anything anyone can ever describe.

"Listen, when he comes out there are going to be a bunch of people in here because he's premature," my doctor explained to me before I started pushing.

"But will I get to hold him?" I asked.

"We're not sure," she said. "We just won't know until after he's out."

That's where the unexpected nature of this whole fiasco really hit home. When you have a healthy pregnancy, you never wonder if you'll get to hold your son right after he's born. It's a given. I was terrified, but I also knew I had to be a soldier. *I have to be as strong as I possibly can*, I thought. *I just have to.*

Just as the doctor had promised, as soon as Jack came out eight to ten people from the NICU appeared. Chris and I held him for a brief moment and he was crying and looked like a minuscule noodle. But he was tall and beautiful and perfect. And just like that they whisked him away to the NICU and I had to deliver the placenta, which I didn't get to see even though I really wanted to. Not because I wanted to grind it up and pop it in pill form but because I like gross things.

Jack was in the NICU for about a month, and I was released from the hospital after day two. For the next four weeks, I spent all day there, pumping milk for my baby until my nipples were bleeding and blistered, because it felt like the only thing I could do to help him. He was fed the milk through a tube up his nose. In that month, we went through the transition where the terror you'd dreaded (or not even dreaded, in my case, because it never occurred to me that I would have a premature baby) becomes your weird normalcy, though every day is peppered with the intense emotional pendulum swings of parenthood, from clouds of disbelief to flashes of reality to moments of pure optimism.

The same group of shell-shocked parents came into the NICU every day and the group of us became an odd community—the kind that no one wants to be a part of, but then you are so grateful to have it. And it certainly made me realize the bubble I lived in. My friends are all in the entertainment industry and I don't leave the house very much, and if I do I go to work or shopping at Barneys or some similarly lame Hollywood shit. But the cross-section of the people in the NICU who were just as scared as we were, it was as intense a reminder as any that the celebrity stuff doesn't really mean anything. We're all just parents trying to raise healthy kids at the end of the day.

On our fourth day in the NICU, the pediatric neurosurgeon sat Chris and me down to tell us that Jack had some severe brain bleeding and there was a chance that he could be developmentally disabled. We wouldn't know until he was eighteen months old, the doctor said. They wouldn't be able to get a true sense of what Jack's development would be like until then. I only half heard the words as they came out of the doctor's mouth. I was in complete shock—somehow, despite everything that had already happened and the fact that, at that point, nothing should have surprised me, I was continually taken off guard.

We went back into soldier mode. There's a shield you build when faced with obstacles like these, largely for your own self-protection and the protection of your child. So Chris and I did what we could, which was hold hands and hope and face it together. We held hands while the doctor spoke, and held hands—and smiled!—as we left the hospital, because we were getting paparazzied every time we left, which, frankly, was horrible. How do you smile when you're spending your days worrying about your sub-four-pound baby? But you don't really have a choice, because if you're frowning, then who knows what the tabloids could say. The last thing you want is a magazine running a false headline about the health of your premature baby. Mostly we just held hands and tried to keep our heads down.

That night, Chris and I went out to eat at a noodle restaurant. We wanted to absorb the information as a team and talk about how we could do this. *Okay, these are the challenges that life throws at you*, we thought. *We've lived these amazing fortunate lives, and this is our moment to step up. There are people who face these kinds of challenges all the time, who don't necessarily have the family or the financial benefits that we do, so we're going to rise to the occasion and attempt to be great parents to the child we love ferociously.*

It was an emotional day, but I felt so strongly that it was important not to cry in front of Chris. I wanted to be as strong as he needed me to be, and as strong as I needed me to be. These moments can be hard on couples, but for us it really brought us together. It felt like it was us against the world.

In the face of that terrifying warning, Chris took on the job of the patriarch, which for sure goes against my feminist sensibilities. But he needed to be the dude in that moment and I was happy to let him. And because we both wanted to wear a brave face, we didn't let ourselves break down in any way. I know it sounds crazy and superficial, but I think being in our industry for so long, and facing so much rejection, taught us how to build an armor. You need it to survive in Hollywood, and you have to be able to say, *Okay, what else are you going to throw at me?*

After a few days, we finally cried and did a lot of what you're not supposed to do—googling potential scenarios and looking for other parents with these particular issues. There were some really helpful stories out there and some not-so-helpful ones, too.

I felt so incredibly close to Chris in those moments. It was all so unexpected, and we knew we might be raising a child who was completely different than we had imagined, and I felt so lucky to have a partner who would be able to rise to the challenge with me. Those days also forced us to have some difficult and candid conversations that, as we thought about maybe expanding our family one day, were necessary. Discussions about high-risk pregnancies and miscarriage and things that no one likes to talk about, but every couple probably should.

When you have a baby in the NICU, every parent has the same question every day: "When can we take him home?" It's what every family wants to know, and the nurses always say the same thing: "We don't know." Jack spent three and a half weeks in the hospital because we couldn't take him home until he could eat on his own. It was an emotionally exhausting month—worrying about Jack and watching nurses poke and prod his gangly limbs with his impossibly tiny diapers that were about the size of a Kleenex. But the silver lining was that the nurses trained me in so many of the tactical parts of parenting. How to swaddle, how to wash bottles, how to bathe a baby—I learned it all at the hospital. I'd never taken care of an infant before, and the nursing staff was a great support system. They were also, in a wonderful way, very practical. They didn't give me any sympathy, and instead were totally direct. *Here's what you'll have to do; here's how to do it.* I was shell-shocked by it at first—why weren't they upset like I was? Couldn't they be a little more sensitive? But in the end their no-nonsense attitude reminded me that there was no room for self-pity. It would have been harder if they had given me a lot of sympathy, I think. It also helped that those nurses tossed Jack around like he wasn't the superdelicate little guy he appeared to be. Their nonchalance about his tinyness made me feel good in a weird way. It was like, *Oh, they don't seem fazed at all, maybe it's not so bad.*

The exact opposite happened when my parents came to meet their grandson for the first time. Long before I went into labor, my parents had planned a trip to Turkey for that August

(Jack was due in October, so it seemed like a perfect time to go away), so they were on a boat when Jack was born. When they got back, Jack was still in the NICU but he was about three weeks old. I was so excited, because he had grown a lot. I was calmer, and I'd gotten used to the NICU routine of pumping and scrubbing and pumping again. I was just thrilled to introduce them to their first grandchild. But after my parents walked into the NICU, my dad saw Jack and he burst into tears in a way that was joyous but also full of concern, and it made me realize how little my baby appeared to strangers and to the family that already had so much love for him.

W hen Jack was four pounds, three ounces, we took him home. Getting the news that he could finally leave reminded me of waiting to get my Cabbage Patch doll when I was young. Finally the call came in—I could go to Toys"R"Us and pick up Rebecca, my brunette Cabbage Patch Kid. I wanted a blond like me, but a brunette is what came, so what can you do? I'd been waiting for her so long, and finally, she was coming to my house.

Jack was an actual, live human being, not a plastic doll, but I took Rebecca really seriously.

We left the hospital as a family on September 12—nearly a month after Jack's August 17 birthday—knowing that we really couldn't know what was coming. It felt so good to put him in that car seat, but also tragic because there were a few parents who we'd become close to who weren't able to take their babies home. On the flip side, we'd already been the parents watching with jealousy as other families left the hospital with their kids. It really was a weird environment.

Even after we got home I was taking Jack to daily appointments with brain specialists and heart specialists and eye doctors and physical therapists. We continued to hope for the best, but we knew that we wouldn't be sure about Jack's development for some time. Still, by the time he reached four or five months old he was incredibly engaging, and by ten months he was superactive. There was nothing about him that seemed checked out. Not that I really knew what I should be looking for—the doctor told us we wouldn't know anything for sure until Jack was about a year and a half. But he was speaking at an early age, and people were constantly telling us how smart he was, which I know people probably say to all new parents, but it took on even more meaning for me. I was constantly seeking reassurance. *You think so? Really?* I wanted to be sure other people were seeing what I was—a kid who seemed largely on track for his age—because I knew better than to trust my own judgment. I am a mom, after all, and what mom doesn't think her baby is a genius?

But our instincts were right, and it turned out that Jack's development was progressing completely on par for his age. Today, he's a happy five-year-old full of wonder and mischief. He still has a couple of physical problems—his legs have high tone and often appear stiff, so he walks on his tiptoes a lot. He wears glasses and has to wear an eye patch for twenty minutes a day to strengthen his vision. But given that these are the biggest challenges, we count ourselves as extremely lucky. There are plenty of parents who walk out of the NICU and don't have as wonderful a story. In fact, premature birth is now the leading cause of death of children worldwide, including in North America. Chris and I have become involved with Healthy Pregnancy 2030, which is working to find ways to prevent preterm and stillbirth, because we know how fortunate we are to have had a happy ending. So the fact that we have a charming and outgoing and athletic kid who loves dinosaurs and introducing himself to people, Chris and I are both grateful every day.

So grateful, in fact, that we find ourselves giving in to things we know we shouldn't. For instance, when I was pregnant, it seemed like all my mom friends had the same advice:

"Do not ever let your child get into the habit of sleeping in bed with you." Chris and I are completely guilty of this. Even now, when Jack crawls into bed next to me, it's hard not to kind of love it. He'll kiss my back or pet me and I am so aware of the fact that in another year or so he'll have no interest in cuddling with his mom, so how could I kick him out?

Today, Jack is at a beautiful age. He has some temper tantrums occasionally (did I mention he's five?) but he's a really

good kid and he's happy and delicious and likes cuddles and I recognize he will not be like this for long.

I think it's foolish for anyone to make major decisions like having a kid without a lot of introspection and examining from all angles and recognizing the complications a child introduces into your life. Because there are times when your kid really bugs you, and there are times you can't do something you want to because you don't have a babysitter. And there are for sure some moments when every parent wonders, *Why did I do this? What do I get out of having children?* I know it's a selfish perspective, but you can't help but think about it every now and then. But it's in those moments early in the morning when I'm listening to Jack giggle, or when his little fat foot starts kicking me in the back in bed, that I remember.

Raising a child in LA, especially for Chris and me, feels so incredibly weird sometimes. Neither of us grew up in this environment, surrounded by wealth and self-centeredness and narcissism. I think that's why it's especially important to both of us that we raise a conscientious child. We want so much for him to be a kind person. That's the big goal. To raise a kind boy who understands that Mommy and Daddy work hard and came to this town not knowing anybody and, granted, we had privileges being white American citizens of Germanic heritage, but still we came here with not a lot at all.

I want Jack to always understand the idea of hard work and perseverance, as cheesy and old-fashioned as that sounds. It kind of flies in the face of LA in general, which is why I think we've been struggling in terms of where we want to raise him. Do we send him to a private school where they raise chickens and build robots out of rubber or whatever the fuck they do, and pay a small fortune? Or do we send him to a public school where he gets exposure to more diversity and the realities of class and racial discrimination? Truth be told, we will probably choose the former because if you have the resources to send your kid to a school where a teacher can teach a class of only seven children rather than thirty how to read, why not do that? It feels a little self-serving to say, "You are going to have the experience that I had," when perhaps we're lucky enough to be able to give him more, or better, than that. I don't want him to have the mediocre high school experience that I did. I don't want him to have to deal with tired teachers and bullies in the locker room. Even though I think that made me stronger, it would be kind of cruel to force it on someone else.

But I shouldn't get ahead of myself. I used to think I might be eager for Jack to grow up a little and be more of a real person, but now he's just graduating toddlerhood, and I didn't think I'd ever say this but . . . I'm kind of mourning it. This stage of his life has been exhausting, chasing a small creature around and making sure he doesn't eat poison or fall down the stairs, but there is definitely some heartbreak in the knowledge that he will never want me around in the way he does now. Soon I'll just be that embarrassing mom who told the world he used to pet me in bed.

# Unqualified Advice:
# Protect Your Heart

**M**y mom always told me to be selfish in love.

She first said it when I was sixteen and I was falling for Chad Burke, when she saw my head spinning off my body with the dizziness of young love. She would repeat it through various stages of my life, and I truly didn't understand what she meant for a long time.

It was a confusing idea, to be selfish in love. Isn't being selfish the opposite of love? Isn't love about generosity and openness of heart?

In hindsight, I think what my mom was saying was that relationships are an area in which you have to look out for your own interests, otherwise nobody is going to be happy. If you take care of yourself, your relationship will be much more successful than if you don't. I understand now that my mother didn't mean don't make dinner for somebody you love, but she meant don't make dinner, clean up, and then do the laundry all the next day and be resentful about it. It meant let somebody do his share and show you generosity, too.

More so than with Chad, the advice to be selfish in love came up with my college boyfriend Dave. I think my mother realized that I wasn't all that crazy about him, but I felt like I couldn't leave him because he needed me so much more than I needed him. Dave and I dated for four years on and off, but I never felt that swoony love for him that I did for Chad. Dave was my dorm stoner buddy. We would listen to 311 all the time and occasionally have sex. I knew that he liked me, and since I didn't have any real friends and he felt like my friend, we dated. It was a very childish relationship. We would smoke weed and go for walks and make each other giggle, but he was not someone I ever felt like I was going to marry, and I don't think he felt that way about me, either.

When I went to study abroad in Italy, I told Dave that I wanted to see other people, but he did that thing where he just said no and refused to accept it. I really didn't know how to lay down the law.

This comes up a lot on the podcast, because oftentimes, as women, we feel the burden of the breakup. *How is this person going to have clean clothes or go to the doctor or literally function in any way without me?* I can relate to that concern, which sadly feels really gender-specific. By the time I got together with Chris, I just wanted a man who could make his own dentist appointment.

I'm not trying to play the martyr. If ever I was taken for granted by men, I bear some of the blame. Getting to that point where I wanted to break up with the guy, but I also worried who would manage his life, was my own doing because I spent a lot of time embracing the caretaker role. So I think my mother told me to be selfish in love as a way of giving me permission to leave a relationship, and I think she was really onto something.

On the podcast, I repeat my mom's advice sometimes, but I've also developed my own mantra—a perhaps gentler version of my mother's: protect your heart.

With "protect your heart," the underlying sentiment is similar to being selfish in love, but there's a key difference. I say protect your heart when someone is calling in about an asshole they're having sex with but aren't really dating, and they're delusional about what the level of commitment is. They want to believe there is more to the relationship than there really is, and I worry that they're setting themselves up for heartbreak.

I tell someone to be selfish in love when they are in a relationship that is clearly bad; I say protect your heart when you're not in a relationship and you are telling yourself you are.

*Be selfish in love* is a kinder phrase for "He's a fucking dick; you've got to get out before you marry this person." *Protect your heart* is a kinder phrase for "He's using you."

I definitely advocate trusting someone and occasionally giving him the benefit of the doubt, but I do think that in the beginning, more than any other time, you've got to protect your heart. A ton of our calls come from young women who are between, say, nineteen and twenty-five, and their story is some variation of "I'm hooking up with this guy and I'm feeling confused about why he doesn't like me as much as I like him." They use varied language to describe this problem, which is one we've all had. And basically all young adults have to go through it before they become a proper human.

There's so much pressure right now to embody a Samantha Jones attitude. *I own my body so entirely that sex is pure physical gratification. I do as I please, whenever I please.* As much as I love *Sex and the City*, maybe we should all agree that Samantha created an urban myth. I admire the idea of sexual freedom, but it's just not in my makeup. I wish it were, but somebody entering my body? I can't stay emotionally uninvested there. We hear callers into the podcast talk about that idea and wanting to achieve it, and I don't blame them, because it means feeling all powerful, but I've yet to talk to anyone who has *actually* achieved it.

Instead, callers tell stories of people (usually men) for whom they are playing the part of the cool, down-with-anything girl, because they don't want to be the emotional aggressor or demand "the talk." And usually these women aren't being honest with themselves. They are saying "I'm okay with it but . . ." when really they aren't, or "I want to give him the time he needs, except . . ." when really they don't. I just want to be straight with them. Don't let yourself be used. Value yourself and value what you bring to the table. And if you're not feeling valued, examine that, because it's painful to have someone not treat you exactly the way you want them to. And if someone is treating you poorly at the beginning of a relationship, I don't see a world where that behavior pattern changes very much. At least, I haven't heard many stories of shitty dudes suddenly becoming wonderful.

So, if someone is showing you who he is—by saying he's not ready to commit, or by explaining the 101 reasons why, even though you are *so great*, he doesn't want to introduce you to his friends—don't ignore it. Decide if this is the kind of person you have the energy for. If you don't want to put up with it, that's you protecting your heart and being selfish in love. And if you decide you're okay with it, that's fine, but don't come crying to *Anna Faris Is Unqualified*.

I'm kidding. Please do. I promise I'll be gentle.

# Listener Advice:
# More Love Mantras

Protect your heart," and "be selfish in love," have served me well. But a great mantra for one person isn't necessarily the guiding light for another. So I was curious what phrases help you guys navigate relationships. Here are your love mantras, as collected on Facebook:

My mom always told me to never chase a man. If they want to be with you then they won't need to be chased.

—Claire

My favorite professor always used the quote "Don't let anyone rent space in your head unless they're a good tenant." I like changing head to heart. It's definitely been something I've tried to follow with every relationship in my life.

—Jenny

---

Be responsible for your own happiness. It's not your partner's job to make you happy, or your job to make them happy.

—Nicky

---

I have, "You cannot save people, you can only love them" tattooed on my rib cage. I'm the type that always wants to take care of people, and it's a reminder to me that not everyone wants to be saved.

—Aleksa

---

Don't do anything you wouldn't want on the front page of the newspaper. Advice from my grandma.

—Krissy

Grandma had three rules on relationships: don't
expect it to be easy, it's work; if anyone starts playing
games with you, leave; and all you ever have to
decide is if you want to see them again—after that
every other decision becomes easy.

—Aaron

If your partner is going to leave you, they will
leave no matter what you do or change about yourself,
so stop stressing, be yourself and love without fear.

—Rebecca

Give your partner space. Room to breathe and
time to be alone for a little bit. It's okay to not do
everything together.

—Susie

A marriage is made up of two really good forgivers.

—Brandi

---

Don't set your partner up for failure by expecting him or her to read your mind.

—Megan

---

The world doesn't revolve around me. Sometimes I've just got to step back and remember that the people I love have their own lives. The only thing I can truly control in a relationship is me.

—Rachel

---

If I wouldn't want it for my kids, I shouldn't put up with it happening to me.

—Megan

---

When it's right, it's easy.

—Lucy

---

My husband's mantra is don't throw it away if you can fix it.

—Audrey

Love is like a piece of glass: hold it too tight and it will shatter; hold it too loose and it will slip away.

—Madison

Don't regret anything! Every choice, no matter how it ends, is a chance to learn and love. Even if love doesn't last forever it was a moment in time. Take what you can from it, reflect, protect your heart, and stay open.

—Stephanie

Be Kind. Be Polite. Be Grateful. My husband and I have been together for 7 years and this has been our mantra. We always say please and thank you to each other.

—Camryn

---

The first time someone shows you who they are, believe them.

—Jennifer

---

Think of a relationship like a bank. Sometimes you make deposits, sometimes you make withdrawals. If one person is always making the deposits and the other is always making withdrawals, the person making deposits eventually runs out. It's rarely, if ever, split 50/50, but both partners need to make deposits as frequently as they withdraw.

—Brianne

---

You are not the exception to the rule, you are the rule. Just because Susie has a sister whose boyfriend's 3rd cousin's fiancé got his shit together for her and they lived happily ever after doesn't mean they all will.

—Nicole

Don't judge them by what they say, judge them by what they do.

—Daphne

You can't change your partner, you can only change yourself. By continually learning about yourself and becoming more aware of your words/actions and how they may affect the other person, you will be able to change the things that you have control over and eventually your partner (or other side of the relationship) will change themselves by reaction to your improvements. You only have control over yourself.

—Dany

I say DO go to bed angry. Much better to come at it with a refreshed rational brain in the morning . . . especially because the tequila has probably worn off by then.

—Laura

What I've learned is that no two relationships are the same. So protect your heart by just doing what's right for you, and don't worry about what everyone else is doing.

—Sarah

Give yourselves the opportunity to miss each other. Obviously spending time together is great, but I think it's really important to not lose sight of who you are as a person aside from being part of the couple.

—Samantha

People in good relationships never stop doing things for each other. Not necessarily big things, but little things. Like scraping their windshield on a frosty morning, starting the coffee machine so it will be ready when they get up, making their favorite dessert or even leaving a little love note somewhere they will come across it.

—Tammy

# Forty

I just turned forty. I didn't think about it much beforehand, because I'm not a birthday person, but aging is such a hot topic in Hollywood that simply surviving another year makes news, especially if you're entering a new decade. That's major. Breaking! Anna Faris had a birthday, again! Didn't she just have one last year? Yup! But this is the big 4-0!

(Part of my ambivalence about my birthday has to do with the actual date. November 29. Growing up in Washington, November is the gloomiest, most depressing time of the year, and my birthday always falls right after Thanksgiving, so everyone is sick of their families. Chris, on the other hand, has the perfect birthday. June 21. It's the summer solstice, school is just out, and everyone is getting ready for summer and celebrating. He just seems like the summer birthday type, doesn't he?)

The most annoying thing about turning forty has most definitely been when people say "Ooooh, the big 4-0." I just don't understand what that means. Am I supposed to be embarrassed? To feel different? It seems like one of those things that is a bigger deal to other people than it is to me, so perhaps I'm not honoring it enough on my end. There's an implication that I'm supposed to be freaking out. But I just don't feel old.

I also don't think I look particularly old, but I don't really know what that means, either. It's always odd when somebody says "Oh my God, you don't look forty," and then they throw out another number. Sometimes it's crazy—"You look like you're twenty-three!"—but more often I'll get "You don't look forty, you look thirty-seven," and I just don't know how to take that. I know it's meant as a compliment, so I guess I'm grateful, but it's also confounding. First of all, in what ways do a forty-year-old and thirty-seven-year-old look different? Are those the key years where wrinkles and general old-bagginess set in? And why is that a thing we're supposed to say to each other? Whenever someone mentions that they're thirty-five or forty or fifty, we automatically default to a compliment that is basically just, "You look great for your decrepit, raggedy age!" What is that about?

I don't want to paint a perfect, or perfectly enlightened, picture around age. There are things about getting older that make me feel crappy, and then I in turn feel crappy about feeling crappy. I'm getting spider veins on the sides of my knees and I've been dyeing my hair for so long that I probably have a head full of grays and don't even know it. Articles seem to note that Chris is younger than me, as if that's a robbing-the-cradle sort of thing because I've got a whopping three years on him. I used to have a cute butt, and now it sags to my knees. I wear sweatpants and boots and grubby T-shirts to work because I rehearse all day, so I constantly have to squash the catcalls. "I don't want anybody telling me how sexy I am today, guys," I'll explain to the crew. "It's too much, I can't handle it."

Despite the spider veins and the maybe-gray hair, the only time I've truly felt old since I turned forty was when I went to the doctor. "You're not twenty, you're forty," she reminded me as she took my blood pressure. "Stop thinking you're twenty." Coming from a doctor, that's the moment when you're like, *Okay, fair point.* So maybe the biological clock part reminds me that I'm not as young as I used to be.

There's also the whole "aging in Hollywood" thing. (Excuse me while my eyes glaze over. . . .) In a recent *Washington Post* article titled WHY THE AGE OF 40 IS SO IMPORTANT IN HOLLYWOOD, the first line reads: "Hollywood is a harsh place for women who dare to age." The article goes on to explain that three-quarters of leading roles for females go to women under forty. The depressing part about this article (because apparently *that* wasn't the depressing part) is that the research shows that Hollywood isn't really changing. "Even as women have become vastly more visible in the workplace, the hiring patterns in Hollywood seem to be stuck in the 1960s," the author explains.

When I got to Hollywood in the late nineties, everyone was lying about their age. Now there's a law that you can't even ask actors about their age, which is a little bit ridiculous. Especially since, in this social media world, you can't really get away with keeping your age quiet. I have generally taken the opposite approach. I talk about my age all the time, especially on the podcast. I guess I feel like the best way to get control over it is by simply owning it. Otherwise your age feels like the elephant in the room. (That said, I make a concerted effort not to ask our female callers their age. Even if it seems relevant to their question, I don't want other women to get sucked into the time-frame shit we've all had to deal with forever.) Am I scared of getting older? Sometimes, sure. Am I scared of people saying I don't look as good as I used to? Fuck yeah. Would I like to have been born in 1992? Okay, I would. But I've got plenty of other things to be grateful for.

I'll be honest: it doesn't feel great to work really hard for nearly twenty years in this town and then worry you won't get hired again because you're no longer fuckable. I would like to think that women want to see a man and a woman of a similar age having a romance. In a moment of insecurity, I have definitely asked Chris: "As you have more and more influence in casting your movies, will you think about someone closer to Rachel McAdams's age?" (She's thirty-eight.) Because today, it's still completely usual to have a fifteen-year difference and nobody bats an eye. As long as the man is the older one, that is.

But I'm not without hope. After a couple of decades in which Hollywood casted quite young, I feel a shift, regardless of what that article says. I'm suddenly getting really nice offers and I like to think that's because of the strength of women at the box office. There are a lot of highly accomplished actresses in my age range who continue to work and act and carry movies. And I do think that simply because I've hung in the game for so long, people realize that I'm not going anywhere. So they think, *We can't get rid of her, might as well work together on some shit.* That's been one of the perks of comedy, too. It allows for women to have longevity. I won't be the leading lady always—I'll become the auntie and the stepmom and mom and then maybe grandma. I'll do all the normal transitions, but if people will still hire me, then I don't mind that shift. There's a lot of liberation in playing supporting characters and not the lead.

Age is also less limiting in today's Hollywood world because actors have the ability to do other creative things. Performers who are ambitious can figure out other avenues: writing or teaming up with a producing partner or writing books or doing podcasts. Seth Rogan and his team are a perfect example of that thought process. *Okay, if they're not going to hire me, how do I generate my own material?* It's what happened to me with *The House Bunny.* I thought, *I'm not sure where my next opportunity will come, so maybe I should just create it.* And so I developed a film about a lovable Playboy Bunny house mom.

There have been some joys in aging. One of the greatest gifts about getting older has been developing a newfound confidence. I feel more comfortable in my skin, and thus more comfortable being self-deprecating and boisterous at the same time. In my twenties, I felt a constant need to prove myself, so any time I was the butt of the joke—even when it was my own doing—I would simultaneously try to remind everyone to take me seriously.

Back then, I hadn't quite figured out what it meant to be a leader, either. I wanted to harness the power I was given on the sets where I was in a prominent position, but I didn't know how to do it right. It actually took Keenen Ivory Wayans delivering a bit of a wake-up call for me to realize how and when to pick my battles. While we were working together on *Scary Movie 2*, there was a senior crew member who I'd heard from friends on set was really hard on his team. He worked them incredibly long hours and didn't seem to care about their wellbeing, and I felt like I potentially had the power to stand up for them. They didn't ask me to do this, but I approached Keenen, who was the creator and director of the movie and told him about the problem. These were people I was rehearsing with every day, it wasn't a group of people I saw for only, like, twenty minutes every now and then. I wanted to fight for them.

"You know what," Keenen said. "I think this is your battle." I was a little stung by that, but I also remember thinking that now if I didn't go to this guy Keenen would know that I was being wimpy and just running to the daddy figure on set. And so the next day I asked the senior crew member if we could talk after lunch. My heart was pounding and I was so nervous (not sure if you know this by now, but confrontation is not my strong suit), but we went for a walk and I said awkwardly, "I feel like you can be really mean to some of the people you work with, and I think you may not realize that I feel it but I do. I really like you and respect you but I'm not sure what else to do at this point." It was one of my first adult conversations and he was awesome about it, thanking me for coming to him and seemingly taking what I said to heart.

Now that I'm reflecting on it, Keenen and this guy were pretty good friends, so maybe he was warned ahead of time. "Anna's going to come to you and say you're mean," Keenen probably said. "Be sweet to her." But he was sweet, and it taught me an important lesson. I was looking to Keenen to be my defender and protector, even though I wasn't the one who needed protecting. I just wanted to assert my power, because I was twenty-three and didn't know better. The senior crew member, on the other hand, was in his mid-thirties, and I was definitely a little intimidated by him. In hindsight, it was a conversation that probably wasn't mine to have as he was never rude to me personally. It was just that I heard from people who were becoming my friends about how cruel he was, and I felt I had the power to make a change.

I don't know how I would handle that situation today, because I'm not sure it was my battle to fight back then, and I don't like to pick a fight just to pick a fight. But I'm grateful to have had that uncomfortable conversation, because those talks are part of growing up, whether it's about leaving your agent or talking to your director or costar or something else completely unrelated to Hollywood. There are many degrees of confrontation that I haven't always known how to navigate in a way that is practical but also forceful enough to ensure I'm heard.

Today, I approach my on-set leadership role very differently. I consider it to be largely my responsibility to create an air of positivity among everyone working on *Mom*. I have a routine on set every Friday, before we tape the show, where I make an announcement to the crew. Now that we're in season five, they all laugh before I even start talking because they know what I'm going to say. It goes something like this: "Hey, everybody, I have an announcement. I just want to tell you guys all how much I love you and what an amazing team we are. You are the best. I feel so lucky that I get to drive to work knowing that I'm going to see you." It's literally the same exact four sentences every week. It sounds so minor, but I would never have thought to do that in my twenties. It wouldn't have occurred to me because I was too self-absorbed to turn the spotlight on other people, and I wasn't comfortable enough in a leadership position to realize that I could use it to establish a positive atmosphere. Plus, I would have worried that everyone was thinking, *Who is this young kid telling us she loves us?* I took myself seriously, because I wanted other people to do the same. Now that I'm older, I know that speech may be stupid, but at least I can own it and laugh at myself. Why not spread the love, even if it means that I come across as an idiot?

And I do like spreading the love. I think I was always a

nice person but I've become more overtly kind as I've aged. I feel more generous. Some people see that as being a pushover, and in some cases my aversion to drama is perceived as weakness, which seems like a weird reaction. People have asked me why I don't stand up for myself more often. But I do when I feel the need to, I just don't feel that need very often. And, in Hollywood, "standing up for yourself" is often code for making unreasonable demands and generally being a diva. I don't need my kale pear juice freshly squeezed and hand-delivered to me every morning, I can get my own juice. That doesn't seem like something that warrants a fit.

There's so much childish coddling of actors in our industry—there's a pattern where actors are treated like children, and therefore behave like children, and that's why there are eight people whose job it is to literally track where we are at all times. It's crazy, because you'd think an adult would know how to be where they're supposed to be, on time, or how to hold their bladder when necessary or be hungry for a minute without needing immediate attention. I know I'm supposed to be on set at 9:00 A.M., and so I should be on set at 9:00 A.M., and someone shouldn't have to knock on my door and say, "Hey, we'd like to invite you to set now." Those are the actual words they use in Hollywood, no matter what you're filming: "We'd like to invite you to set." It's kind of ridiculous. So I don't think the fact that I don't need everything on demand makes me a pushover, I think it makes me a self-sufficient adult.

A common theme of hitting a certain age, especially among

women, is the tendency—or at least the desire—to be a bit tougher and give up on the people pleasing. But the reality is that I struggle with being a people pleaser, and I don't think that's something I can change in myself. I like to think I'm shifting away from the constant need to be liked, but sometimes I enjoy doing things because they will make other people happy. I want to give a compliment just because I do, not because I'll get anything in return. Which isn't to say I'm not vain and I don't love hearing nice things said about me—of course I am and of course I do. But giving other people small moments of pleasure, I get a kick out of it.

Looking back at my thirties, they were definitely a time of great growth and an influx of confidence and happiness—I married Chris and had Jack and joined *Mom* and started my podcast. It felt like my career had a different kind of resurgence, one that I actually had some control over, with movies like *The House Bunny* and *What's Your Number?* My twenties were about projects like *Scary Movie* and *The Hot Chick*, in which I had zero creative input. I was along for somebody else's ride. But in my thirties, I got to have more creative control, or maybe it was just that I was more proactive and people took me more seriously. I don't know, but it was great. So I hope that in my forties I get to continue on that path. I'd like to produce more, too, so I'm hoping that those doors will open and interesting roles will present themselves as well.

But more interesting than my forties, I think, is thinking about when I'm sixty and imagining what that looks like. I'd like to live in Washington and I'll have built a little amphitheater—well, John the artist down the street will have built it, but I'll have cheered him on—and have a grumpy pet pony who bites sometimes but loves me anyway. And I'll channel Annette Bening, who is the most stunning almost-sixty-year-old in existence. My strategy will be to fake it till I make it and just be brimming with sexual confidence. I've got twenty years to get there.

# Unqualified Advice:
# How to Tune Out the Noise

One of the most common issues that Sim and I hear from callers into the podcast has to do with dealing with outside pressure—to get married, to have a kid, to have a second kid, whatever it is. We had one caller, Bree, who had recently finished her PhD. She was the only person in her family to graduate college, let alone to get an advanced degree, and she was also a successful dance teacher. But all Bree's husband's family cared about, she said, was whether she was going to have a baby. She and her husband—who happened to be her high school sweetheart—had agreed they didn't want kids, but the incessant questions from her in-laws were pissing her off, and making her question her husband's happiness in their marriage.

The call made me sad for a number of reasons, mostly because I know that so many women deal with that kind of pressure every day. For me, it's the question of a second kid. I get it mostly from the press. I'm an easy red-carpet target if

I'm out with my family. It's so obvious for a journalist to say, "I saw the cutest Instagram of you with your son, Jack; are you going to have another?" Part of me wants to just say, "Please fuck off," but I try to be straightforward in those conversations. So I just say, "I would love to have more kids," and if I'm feeling saucy I'll say, "but I'm getting up there!" just to make myself laugh, and because it makes people uncomfortable once you bring age into it. That's when then they realize that, *Oh, maybe I've intruded too much.*

There's no question that women are strapped to a timeline, and one that is largely dictated by outside forces. The silver lining, if you really look for it, is that "the timeline" can make you even more career-driven and focused, cultivating an eye-on-the-prize mentality that was a benefit to me. But the downside is that when you're with your boyfriend of seven years, people are like, "When are you going to put a ring on it???"

First of all, it's weird to call someone an "it." But also, maybe you don't want to get married. Or maybe you're not in a rush.

I've gotten better at tuning out the noise as I've gotten older, but I've definitely been guilty of falling victim to "the timeline." In my twenties, I demanded a timeline from everything in my life. It helped me hustle around this town and get work, but it also led me to a marriage that I shouldn't have been in. It's so odd that men don't have that same pressure. Or maybe some do, but for them it's probably more career-based. But the stoner dudes I grew up with in Seattle? Our conversations were like:

**Me:** Are you going to class?

**Stoner Dude:** I don't know.

**Me:** It's starting right now.

**Stoner Dude:** Yeah . . . I don't know.

**Me, internally:** Make up your mind already! I can't deal
with your indecision.

The major fear with "the timeline," and the outside pressure to conform to it, is that you could end up warping yourself and conforming to another person's agenda. Then you'll
inevitably feel frustrated when you aren't getting what you
truly want.

Imagine if every other day different people asked you: "When
are you going to Madagascar? When are you going to Madagascar? But seriously, have you decided when you're going to
Madagascar? So wait, when? When are you going to go?"

Suddenly you're like, "I didn't even know I wanted to,
but . . . maybe I do. Yeah, I guess pretty soon. I'm going on
the trip of my dreams. I'm saving up for Madagascar!"

So we need to maintain perspective, but I don't think there's
an easy way to tune out the noise. If someone asks you, "Soooo,
what are you thinking about kids?" You could always pull a
highbrow cultural analysis, saying, "Have you ever thought
about how there seems to be a timeline for women that doesn't
exist for men? Why do you think that is?" You know, make
people uncomfortable with your clever sociological conun-
drums. But the truth is that I don't think there's a snappy answer
for those intrusive questions, and it's a fruitless effort to try and

stop them entirely. You can't change other people, and it's so ingrained in our culture that calling them out will only make you both uncomfortable. So I think the answer is just having people in your life that you trust, and having friends who love and support you—ones you can talk to about this stuff, because having a dialogue helps relieve the pressure.

Or you can self-deflect like I do and just say, "I know! I'm getting old! Maybe my vagina's just not tight enough anymore to hold a baby."

# Friday, January 6, 2017

**8**:07 A.M.: Woke up with a jolt because I forgot to set my alarm and Jack has to get to school and he's still asleep. Normally, he crawls into bed with me around four, so I get up and drink tea while he snoozes in my bed. Today I get him up, and he groans and then responds to my nudges with a toot in my face. Not sure when Jack's breath and flatulence started smelling like a grown-up's but we've crossed that bridge. (Chris snuck out early to work out and head to a day of meetings, so I don't see him.)

**8:30:** Jack's nanny took him to school since I was running late. I'm not a breakfast person—I'll eat some cereal sometimes, but I really don't care for breakfast food. I would have a turkey sandwich or a burger for breakfast every day if I could. On show days—we tape *Mom* on Friday evenings—I get amped and the nervous energy kind of kills my appetite. Usually I'm a late-night eater. When Chris is gone I'll watch Netflix in bed and eat a giant bowl of pasta with oil and cheese, which I love. When he's here, I get a little embarrassed chomping down on an entire meal at ten thirty.

**9:56:** Just took an "exercise" walk around the neighborhood, which I haven't done in a long time. I wore a cute workout outfit, so it looked like I was really working out but instead of making it the full four miles I called it at a half mile.

**10:03:** I should be looking at my script and calling my dad and my manager and showering but I'm watching old episodes of *Louie*. Man, it's good.

**10:20:** I take quick showers but I love my getting-ready time—especially drying my hair, because that's when I read the newspaper. I've got extensions (a lovely perk of having a child is thinning hair), which take a long time to dry, so on really busy days this feels like my only quiet personal time.

**10:56:** Headed to Warner Bros., stage 20. It's still a thrill to be able to park on the lot instead of walking on holding pages for an audition.

**11:10:** Arrive at work for show-taping day. We tape in front of a live studio audience, which is fun but adds an element of nerves to taping days. (I don't really know how to take a selfie, but here I am wearing a down jacket because in LA people do that when it's sixty-two degrees.)

*I'm scared. I'm always scared.*

**11:15:** Allison is here early, too! Always love seeing her. We get our coffee and gossip instead of rehearsing our lines like we should.

**12:05:** Our sweet but very anxious PA is pacing back and forth, which is making me crazy.

**12:31:** About to start camera blocking for the show. I give myself a solid B for knowing my lines. But I've still got a few hours before we tape.

**1:10:** Bathroom break. Not that exciting.

**1:16:** Allison is taking a bathroom break now. She says she won't share any details.

**2:50:** In the middle of a run-through with the producers. It's superstressful because it's our final rehearsal, but I have a scene off, so I'm writing this. Also, my hair is green, so I have to go get it dechlorinated during my break. (Bleach blondes will understand.)

**3:05:** Finished run-through with producers and writers. It's a nervous time for everyone, but it was successful. I didn't fuck up once!

**3:15:** Headed to hair and makeup to get patched up.

**4:00:** It's our dinner break and I've got a fried chicken salad but I'm too anxious to eat much, even though it's delicious. I've done enough tapings at this point that you'd think it would be second nature, but I still get nervous every week.

**5:36:** Chris and Jack are here! It's the first time Jack has come to a live taping—he's most interested in the coconut cake on the craft service table. It's hard to get him to be polite to my coworkers but he's doing his best.

**6:00:** The actors huddle in hair and makeup with the script supervisor and do the whole show as fast as we can without our script. Depending on people's levels of preparedness, sometimes it's rocky and sometimes it's ten minutes. It's never longer than a half hour, then they hustle us straight to our intros to the live studio audience. The announcer calls our names and we run out and say hello to the crowd, who is usually really welcoming. That helps establish the energy, but it's also when the anxiety of the show starts to hit.

**6:30:** Start taping! I always say doing TV, especially a multi-cam sitcom like *Mom*, is like doing a really fun version of the SATs. It requires a different kind of mental concentration. You only get two shots, because we only really do two takes for each scene. It's somewhere between improv, which is only one shot but tedious in its own way, and a single-cam show, like *Parks and Rec*, in which they do ten to twenty takes.

**9:30:** We used to have big parties with the cast and crew in my dressing room after each taping, but I think now that we're in season four we've all sort of grown out of that. Tonight I'm too tired after the taping to hang out, so I head home. Chris and Jack went home about halfway through, and Jack is already asleep when I get back.

**10:00:** Every Friday night I get the script for the show we'll start working on next week, which feels completely overwhelming but also exciting. I usually stay up late on Fridays to see what's coming up and to get ready for the process to start all over again with Monday's table read. We have rehearsals on Tuesday and Wednesday, and on Thursday we do preshoots—scenes that take place outside or are especially emotional or difficult to tape in front of a live audience. Mondays and Tuesdays I come home and go straight to podcasting, which is wonderful but of course means I can't exercise or take Jack to the park or do anything for myself. It's a passion project but also time-consuming.

**11:00:** I usually go to bed pretty early—Fridays are my late night. It takes me a minute to mentally wind down, so I wash my face and watch *Real Housewives* and basically zone out until I crash.

# She Said, He Said: What It's Like to Be a Couple in Hollywood

Chris and I have been working actors for as long as we've known each other. We've shared the spotlight plenty, and there have been times when one of us stepped aside to let the other one have their moment. It's probably not unlike what happens in most relationships, just on a more public scale. We talked about navigating Hollywood as a couple.

**Anna:** I guess I was the more well-known of us when we first met, though I've never really felt all that famous. But when we first started dating, you were not quite as successful as you are now. I knew you would be, though. I was taken by your talent immediately, because I'd never worked with anyone as good as you. The only other person who struck me like that was Ryan Reynolds—when we did our scenes together in *Just Friends* or *Waiting . . .* , I

would think, *He's making me rise to the challenge.*
But you and I were playing boyfriend and girlfriend,
so it was a romantic scenario on-screen and,
obviously, eventually off-screen, too. In *Take Me
Home Tonight* there was that scene where we were
supposed to kiss, and you suggested that I leap up
onto you and straddle my legs around you and I
did it—and I'm really self-conscious about that sort
of thing—and you slapped my ass a bit. I was so
struck by your confidence. I couldn't believe you
just went for it like that. It was totally appropriate,
because we were playing characters at a high
school party who had been together for a couple of
years, but you were taking control of the scene in a
way that I completely admired. I also found it
terrifying. I was mystified by you. So, the point is,
you weren't a household name yet, but I knew it
was coming.

Chris:  Well, thank you. I remember there was a moment a
while back when a friend of mine who worked in
social media put my name into something that was
like a "star meter" and it said the most famous I'd
ever been at that point was when I got engaged to
you. Our engagement made my star meter go up, or
something, and I remember him laughing and
thinking that was so funny. And it did make me feel
a little weird, if I'm being honest. At that point, the
most fame I'd ever seen was when I did the fourth

season of *The O.C.* I'd managed to be a working
actor but I didn't have any notoriety or real
recognition from it. I was early on in my career at
that point, and mine began totally differently
than yours did. You crushed it right away and hit it
big right out of the gate. I didn't have that. And
there were definitely moments when I felt like
Jason Segel's character in *Forgetting Sarah Marshall*,
like the boyfriend who held the purse on the
sidelines and people didn't really see me. Not that
you ever made me feel like that, it was the people
you introduced me to. Actors would have their
hands all over you and call you babe and you would
say, "This is my boyfriend, Chris," and I'd get a
quick head nod and then they'd turn back to you.
But that's the nature of Hollywood, to be honest.
Relationships here have an element of mutual
benefits to them, so even in social interactions there
is that question of "How can this person help me?"
In that sense, people gravitated more toward you
because you meant more to their dreams. You were
a star.

What's funny is that more than being annoyed
about that treatment, I just kind of felt like
they weren't in on it yet. I've always been weirdly
overconfident, so I thought, *Okay, that's cool.
There's going to be a day when I've had more success
and I'm going to remember these moments and these people.*

**Anna:** That's how I felt when I first met you. Like I was in on something. I was proud of myself for that. Like, I finally have good taste in men, but also I knew I saw something that everyone else would, too, and it was just a matter of time. I give myself a lot of credit for seeing it before everyone else did. Like that opening scene of *Guardians of the Galaxy*, when you are dancing with so much joy? I saw that and thought, *Oh my God, that is so fucking cool and fearless.*

**Chris:** But I saw your star continue to rise after we got together, too. It wasn't like you were some has-been. You had done *Scary Movie*, but not *The House Bunny*, so watching that happen was great. You were pitching it all over town, not just to star in it but to produce it. I couldn't believe it when it happened. It was so cool to watch somebody take an idea and find a partner and go out on the town and get something made. I'd only heard about that, never actually seen it, so to watch it firsthand—I was so impressed.

I get questions from journalists a lot asking how we deal with each other's success. People are curious. It's a natural instinct to assume that the competitive nature of what we do would translate to resentment of each other's careers and even resentment in our lives together, but the good news is that—and I guess I can only speak for myself—but I think we both have pretty impenetrable egos.

**Anna:** I don't know. Sometimes I feel like I don't have the
career that I used to, and I do have moments of
insecurity about that. I'm so thrilled and grateful
that you are doing the things you are, and I have
crazy pride in the fact that your talents are
recognized, but it can be hard not to have a moment
of self-doubt when my husband is acting with young
women in big movies and I'm playing a role in *Mom*
that, while I love it, is incredibly unsexy.

**Chris:** I felt that way when I auditioned for *What's Your
Number?*. I really wanted to play the role Andy
Samberg was cast in and instead I got Disgusting
Donald. And I tested for the Chris Evans role! But
the truth is, in the grand scheme of things, you
might feel that self-doubt in this exact moment, but
it's going to be a blink of the eye and this will all be
over. That's why it's important for both of us to
keep our feet on the ground, because this is all
going to go away one day, and the torch will be
passed. If we're lucky we get one second of success,
and some people get two or three, but it all comes
crashing to a halt eventually, because fame and
notoriety—it's all fake. You have to keep your eye
on the prize, because it's all an illusion.

**Anna:** Of course that's true, and that's very rational of you.
And I am really happy to celebrate your celebrity.
Like when we're in a restaurant, and someone asks
to take a picture with you and hands me the camera,

mostly I love it. The arrogant part of me thinks,
*I found somebody who I saw complete potential in*
*and I'm so proud of him and proud of myself for*
*knowing before everyone else*—see how I make it
about me?—and the vain part of me is happy not to
be in anyone's Facebook photo when I'm in my
sweats and no makeup. And the good-person part of
me thinks it's nice to be able to make a fan's day
with a quick photo. But truth be told, it's not like
I don't walk away with, say, 4 percent of a sting.
It's not much at all, but I wouldn't want the dear
readers of this book to think I'm immune to it
when, after the fact, the people in the picture are
like, "Oh! We like you too! . . . But we don't
really want your photo." It would be dishonest to
pretend that no part of me has a moment of
questioning myself—"Does this mean I'm
irrelevant?"—even though I really would much
rather take the photo than be in it. That doesn't
mean I feel any resentment toward you. I don't. I've
gotten such joy in watching your crazy ascension to
stardom, and mostly I get a kick out of it. I don't
know. It's a great industry to be in for a number of
reasons but it also really messes with your head
sometimes.

**Chris:** Well, the photo thing is just weird, and we've both
had that. You're kind of damned if you do and
damned if you don't, especially when we're

together. If you assume that someone wants you in the photo, you're weird and kind of full of yourself. If you assume they don't, you run the risk of them saying, "Get in!" which can also be awkward. The only right way to deal with it is to be patient and polite and do what you can to smile and be grateful and then keep moving.

Anna: I like to think that plenty of couples deal with these same issues, don't you think? Not the picture-taking, necessarily, but there are always moments when one half of the couple has the spotlight a little more than the other. Whether it's career success or a personal achievement, there have to be moments when it might take a little bit of checking your ego to let the other person have their glory, and not say, "What about me?"

Chris: Yeah, but I think you just focus on what you can control. Keep working hard. Things change in an instant—in our industry, you can look at people who just a few years ago were everywhere, and now that's not the case. So I think for any couple, you just have to remember that the only thing inevitable is change and all you can do is not compare yourself to anybody else. Focus on everything in your control to make that change be something that is moving toward making you better. We're in show business, so for us it's our career or our ability as actors, but for other people it might be something else. But change is coming, so how do you make it a good change? It's all about how you feel about something. If it's good, enjoy the good because you know it could go away any minute, and if it's bad, celebrate the fact that that's going away soon, too.

# Unqualified Advice:
# I Don't Know What I'm Talking About,
# but Here's Some Other Free
# (Or Only the Cost of This Book)
# Unqualified Advice

I seem to have thoughts on everything (dating-related or not, really), so I wanted to gather a few more bits of advice here. These don't warrant their own chapter, I don't think, but think of it like my little compendium of unqualified theories.

## ON SNOOPING

All signs point to me being a snoop. I'm a curious person who wants to hear other people's stories and problems and life plans. But one thing I've learned from friends who have dealt with it is that snooping is always the worst idea. Not a bad idea. *The worst* idea.

I must have had some inkling of this even as a child. You know how some kids rifle through the usual hiding spots to get an early glimpse of their Christmas gifts? That wasn't me. I knew where my mom kept the presents, but I never looked. I don't think I ever really dug much into my parents' things at all. (Note to self: send this chapter to Mom.)

That's not to say I'm necessarily respectful of people's privacy, I just want to hear their business from their own mouths.

I bring this up because so many of the calls into our podcast start with "I know I shouldn't have, but I peeked at his text messages . . ." or "My friend looked through her husband's emails. . . ." So this is my public service announcement: just don't do it.

I get why it's enticing. Especially now, in a world where there are so many places where you can snoop. When I was a kid, we didn't have Facebook or email or text messages. You couldn't log into someone's secret Tinder account or check their call log. You could only listen in on landline phone conversations or read someone's letters. It wasn't like it is today, where as soon as you earn enough trust that someone tells you their password, you can use that against them.

Here's the thing about snooping: it can only lead you to bad places. Either you find out something you don't want to know, or you find out something exciting—he bought a ring!—and then you've ruined the surprise. There's no good outcome. If you think your boyfriend is cheating on you, for example, *not* finding an email to another girl isn't going to convince you he's faithful. It'll probably just convince you he has a secret email account. Like I said, no good outcome.

When Chris and I first moved in together, I didn't even

want to go through his pockets when I was doing his laundry. Not that I suspected him of anything, I just knew that the curiosity could lead me down a path I didn't want to travel. What if some girl at the gym gave him her number and he threw it in his pocket to be polite? I'd probably think he was cheating on me. So I made a policy that I just don't look.

Here's the other thing about snooping: as soon as you get found out, you've lost most of your power in the relationship, whether it's a romantic one or a friendship or family. And if you're in a girlfriend-boyfriend situation, that will always hang over you. It will be ammo the other person will use against you, should it come to that.

Protect yourself. Don't snoop. And when Christmas comes, find a better hiding place.

## THE SIXTY-FORTY RULE

People say that relationships should be an equal partnership. But it's rare that a relationship is ever actually fifty-fifty, even a friendship. A healthy balance, I think, is more like sixty-forty. There's always going to be someone who needs something different from what you need, sometimes more, sometimes less. You probably won't ever both give and get the same amount.

The good news, as I see it, is that the sixty-forty fluctuates. Sometimes you're the sixty; other times you're the forty. But you need to always feel one of two ways: either (1) I think I'm giving more than I'm getting right now, but just a little bit more, and what I'm getting still makes me feel really good. Or (2) I know I'm asking for a lot right now, and I don't have time to give of myself in the same way, but that will change soon and I'll step up.

The important thing to remember is that there's no end to any of it. There's no *I did my part, I'll take it easy now.*

While it's normal for relationships to stray from fifty-fifty, they really should stay at sixty-forty. If yours goes to seventy-thirty or eighty-twenty, it's potentially doomed. That's the relationship orange alert. (The different colors of terror threats are basically impossible to remember. Orange is the "high" alert, FYI. I know that because I just googled it. Red is "severe." What are we supposed to do when we get a red alert? I don't see how knowing we're on severe terror alert is helpful other than inspiring widespread panic. I guess that's why I don't work in national security.)

We talk to a lot of people on the podcast who have veered into seventy-thirty territory. They admit that they're unhappy the majority of the time, and they blame themselves for it. I always think that maybe those people should take a closer look at their relationship and why they're feeling such a high level of inequality. If you're doing all of the childcare and the housework and holding a job, but the other person makes you feel good, then great. That's awesome. But if you're doing all that, and you get nothing in return—no help, and also no good feelings—then that relationship probably won't, and shouldn't, last.

## SPOTTING A CHEAT

Here's a line I've heard three times from three different guys: "I just want to tell you, something happened last night. Amanda/

Sarah/Brandi/Whoever tried to kiss me. I told her no, I'm in a relationship, but I just thought you should know."

Translation: "I fucked Amanda/Sarah/Brandi/Whoever."

At least, that's my theory.

"She tried to kiss me" is a preemptive manipulation tactic to get ahead of any rumors that might start swirling. It's a perfect way for the cheating guy to divert attention away from himself and pit woman against woman instead. It's a strategy that's not unrelated to all the terminology we use to set up women as villains: mistress, home-wrecker, gold digger. (See: *Teen Mom, Teen Mom 2,* and so on. I love these shows. My mom is appalled by them and by the fact that I watch them, but they really are the best birth control.)

It's easy to believe the "she tried to kiss me" line, if you want to. I know, because I've been in the position of believing ridiculous stories when it was easier than facing the truth. Take the summer before college, when I was hanging out in a car, getting stoned with Chad Burke and some other kids, when this gal said, "Ugh, I did not sleep at all last night because I was mashed up against Chad's wall." We were all so high that I don't think she realized what she said until the long awkward silence that followed. Suddenly she looked at me with wide eyes that screamed, *What the fuck did I just say?* I broke out of my stoner brain just long enough to think, *Great, everyone knew that Chad is screwing this girl except me?* But I never confronted him about it. I didn't want to feel like a fool, and I remember sort of wanting to believe that maybe she just didn't have a place to sleep. I didn't want to accept that he was cheating because I didn't want to deal with what that meant, which was that I'd probably have to break up with him. In cheating scenarios, you have to weigh the punishment to yourself against the punishment to the other person, and I didn't want to deal with what I'd be doing to myself—ending the relationship with a shitty guy who I had some kind of cult worship for.

There have been other times when I've believed the "she tried to kiss me" line because, again, it seemed easier to believe a lie than to act on the truth. But the reality is that while there are aggressive women, how many women do you know who actually try to kiss a guy out of nowhere? Especially one they know is in a relationship? *Oh, you found yourself alone outside, smoking a cigarette, and she lunged at you out of nowhere and you said, "I'm sorry, I could never betray my girlfriend"? And then you thought you should tell me because it was just the right thing to do?* I call bullshit. You should, too.

## GO TO BED ANGRY

This was the best piece of relationship advice my brother ever gave me. He was going through a tough breakup a long time ago, and he'd been with someone whose relationship mantra was to never go to bed angry. While that relationship was ending he said to me, "Anna, just go to bed angry. It's fine." And he was so right.

In general, I think women like quick resolutions and for a fight to be over as soon as possible. It's never comfortable to go to bed with an unsettled feeling or with disagreements unresolved. But men, in my experience, need to work off their testosterone, maybe with a hard workout or a night of sleep. Trying to negotiate a fight quickly does not always benefit both parties, and rushing through an issue is not always the best solution.

That's not to say I don't believe in talking things out, but you need to wait until a little time has passed. In the moment, there is too much irrationality, and that's when the really damaging things are said that cannot be taken back. So give each other a little space and go to sleep, even if you're pissed off. Let time do some of the healing.

# This Is the Chapter
# That Will Make You Vomit

I've been witness to romantic gestures big and small all my life. My dad is a romantic guy, and he and my mom were never shy about putting their love on display. My brother, Bob—same thing. And I wouldn't be honoring my relationship with Chris if I didn't acknowledge that he was great at grand gestures but also stellar at the tiny ones. And I think both can have equal impact. I decided to list my most favorite of these gestures—those I've received and those I've seen exchanged between people I love—all in one place; so you can just skip this chapter altogether if it makes you want to puke. But before you do, let me give you one caveat: While I'm conscious of the fact that this kind of sentimentality might be rare, I think every man has his own way of showing love. So while your partner may not display his affection by doing your hair, make a point to notice whatever it is he does that makes you feel special.

## 1. BRAIDING HAIR

My mom loves to French braid my hair. It's a weird thing she does even now that I'm an adult. But she always starts a little too high and I end up looking like a sister wife. Three or four years ago, Chris was watching her do a French braid and wanted to learn. He already knew how to do a regular braid because his sister taught him when they were kids, and he's into knots in general, from being an outdoorsy guy. I know it's weird for someone to be "into" knots, but, for example, he loved it when I had a tangled piece of jewelry. I don't have the patience for de-tangling necklaces, but Chris finds it satisfying, or meditative, I guess. He also loves doing a Rubik's Cube, which is not the same at all but somehow seems related. So anyway, he started giving me French braids. We'd be in bed at night watching football and he'd say, "Let me braid your hair," and I would sit between his legs and let him do my hair. He was always the instigator. It hap-pened less as I got older because I've had a lot of hair issues and I have extensions so it's harder and less satisfying and I have weird lumps in my scalp, but I still got braids from time to time. Just check Chris's Instagram, where he bragged that "real men braid."

He cuts Jack's hair, too. They play barber together. Chris is a great caretaker in general, but especially when it comes to hair.

## 2. SPEAKING OF HAIR . . .

My mom has cut my dad's hair since he was in the army, in 1970. Doing an army cut was easy, but she's kept up with it since, through plenty of hairstyles. My dad sits in the kitchen in his underwear, and she carefully cuts what remains of his hair, and it's oddly intimate and romantic. Then she sweeps up the floor while he showers and shampoos.

It's funny, because I also remember wandering into the kitchen as a kid every three weeks and smelling bleach, because my father would be bleaching my mother's hair at the kitchen counter. What is it about hair?

My parents have always been very adoring toward each other, with tons of pet names—precious angel, dreamboat, Mrs. Drewbowski (I have no idea where that came from), darling pies—and my dad constantly telling my mom how beautiful she is. She gets embarrassed by it, but it's a wonderful gesture, and one I was lucky to grow up around.

## 3. POEMS, LETTERS, AND OTHER HANDWRITTEN NOTES

Chris wrote me poems and sent me letters from wherever he was in the world, on hotel stationery. So I'd get a letter from a gorgeous hotel in Moscow, or Paris, or wherever work took him, though he was usually home by the time they arrived. They were like old-timey war letters that said things like, "Honey, I'm dreaming of the day I get to hold you again." For such a dude, he's really thoughtful.

He's also a really good artist, and drew me pictures on our mirror. About a year and a half ago, he drew a picture of himself on our bathroom mirror with a love note, and the picture looked remarkably like him. He also wrote me a long poem once that was framed in our home.

Do you want to throw up yet?

## 4. BIG RISKS

My brother, Bob, is a believer that real romance lies in big moves—ones that are risky, costly, and could easily backfire but that leave you transformed either way. When he and my sister-in-law were dating, he decided to surprise her with a trip to Oahu during what he describes as a "rocky period" in their relationship. I know that whisking someone away to Hawaii sounds foolproof on the surface, but they were already going through a rough patch, so this was the kind of trip that could make or break them. Bob mistakenly booked what turned out to be a shitty hotel on Waikiki Beach—think wilted microwave sausages and freeze-dried eggs served on Styrofoam plates. Not the romantic healing getaway he was hoping for. It was turning into one of those risks that didn't pay off, until Bob was able to convince the hotel he had a "family emergency," get a refund on their prepaid stay, and transfer to a beautiful, romantic hotel. They had a magical four days driving around the island, picnicking and swimming on secluded beaches. Now they're married with a beautiful baby girl. I've always been touched by that story, because that kind of big bet is scary when it comes to relationships. He put it all on the line, and I'm so glad it paid off.

## 5. FLOWERS

Every Friday before *Mom* tapings, Chris sent me a giant bouquet of flowers at the studio. I'll admit that sometimes I felt
almost embarrassed, not because I wanted to hide them, but I
didn't want to always be the "look what I got!" girl who rubbed
her romantic husband in her coworker's faces. But yeah, a giant bouquet of flowers in my dressing room wasn't bad.

# Don't Call It Closure

I started seeing a therapist after I began writing this book. I was raised thinking therapy was for the self-indulgent or mentally ill (I could be both); but reexamining my life and revisiting past loves and getting ready to publicize those experiences—all that has dug up a lot of shit, which shouldn't come as too big of a surprise. I thought I was revealing my stories to help other people feel less alone, but instead it has inspired a hearty dose of introspection that I think has bene-fited me. At least, that's what my new therapist, who's very positive and friendly and knows everything about football and always tells me I'm "doing great," says. (At her hourly rate, I have to believe her.)

Though this book is largely about relationships, it has forced me to examine so many different aspects of my life. Somehow this whole journey has made me want to do more—Broadway! Producing! It has stoked my ambitions in a way I never expected. I recently filmed a remake of *Overboard*, and while it may sound dramatic to say that it changed me, it really did. The work was incredibly difficult, but I was able to do all kinds of improv and I felt giddy the whole time. It was so creatively rewarding.

Life is messy. I obviously don't have all the answers. When I first started thinking about writing this book, I pictured myself sitting on my bed with a cup of coffee, all *La la la la la, here's something funny I thought about yesterday, is it funny to you?* It became much more than that. In the end, I hope that it has made some people laugh and made other people feel like they're not crazy, or at least that they're just as crazy as I am so they know they're not alone. So to all of you out there who dedicated time to reading this book . . . well, the phrase "I'm not worthy" is bouncing around in my head. It would be really fucked-up if it weren't, though. If writing a book about yourself is completely natural and easy and you don't have a moment where you wonder, *Why would anyone care?*, then you've drunk way too much of your own Kool-Aid.

If there's one thing I'm grateful for, it's that this book is called *Unqualified*. I don't have everything figured out, and I don't think I ever will. I couldn't even conceive of the feeling of being qualified. Feeling unqualified is in my build. It's hard-coded in my DNA. I'll never not feel fear when I put myself out there, but that's okay. I'll keep doing things I have no right to do, because I don't like wading in the shallow end. I'd rather get pushed into the deep end and then attempt to touch the bottom. That's just how I operate.

Remember the orange ceremony? My attempt at closure with Jason Sprott, the fastest boy in the third grade, where I wrote his name on an orange and threw it into the forest? These days, I take comfort in the belief that there's no such thing as closure. As my family is evolving, I hope we can still have barbecues and Fourth of July celebrations, and that we can proceed forward with love and tenderness.

There is no finish line when it comes to relationships, and I think the search for one will just make you frustrated. So I have no illusions that this book is done and now I can close the door on my past. I do feel like this book is done so . . . let's keep moving and focus on the future. I'm excited to see what will come next. Because a great family and career isn't the end, either. There's always work to be done.

But the thing that writing this book has really taught me, above all else, is how limited my vocabulary is. When I read other people's books or the newspaper in the morning, all I can think is, *Fuck, I know, like, three hundred words.* So I hope you've enjoyed those words. Or at least the 299 of them that weren't *fuck.*

# Acknowledgments

As I sat down (after eating a burger) to write this final portion of the book, my cousin sent me a video of my son, Jack, and his daughter Lillianna spraying packed suitcases with a garden hose. My cousin is with Jack for the weekend while I'm on set shooting a movie, and that video made me realize that the career I've chosen has far-reaching consequences. My child, and my family, will always be affected by the career I've had, for better or for worse, and so I owe a tremendous amount of gratitude to them for never complaining about the strange existence we lead, which will forever impact their lives. Thank you, Bob and Addie, Loren and Megan, Angie and Scott, Owen and Eric, Cully and Brandy, Steve and Teri, Cannon, and Dee and Howard. Thank you, Kathy. Thank you, Kate. I know sometimes it's awesome to have famous people in the family and sometimes it's really hard. And I'm not sure I ever took that into consideration as I pursued my dreams. But here we are, and you've never complained, only supported. And I'm so, so thankful. Because I couldn't have done this without you. Some of you will get thanked again, but for different reasons. I love you all so much.

I would next like to thank my listeners. I'm so lucky to have an audience who truly seems to care as passionately about others as they do themselves. You guys have given me so much.

Thank you also to my unbelievable publishing team at Dutton. (I still can't believe this is happening!) Jill Schwartzman, you wonderful woman you, your belief and support from the very beginning has just meant the world to me. Thank you for your patience, wisdom, and kindness. Also thank you so much to Marya Pasciuto, Amanda Walker, Liza Cassity, and Elina Vaysbeyn. One day, if people read this book, I want to adultnap you all and take you to Bora Bora. Four Seasons. Let's do it.

Rachel! Rachel Bertsche! I couldn't love you more. I'm so happy you came into my life—you are so brilliant and incredible. Without you none of this would be happening, and I know we will be friends for life because I will be pestering you for the rest of time. You have taught me so much about life and love and friendship, and I couldn't be more grateful. (Have you considered becoming a therapist?)

Sim Sarna. Sim, what a dear friend. You've turned my little idea into a passion project and I'm so grateful. Cassie Daniels and Amy Pomerantz: I'm so lucky to have such brilliant women in my life. Thank you.

Thank you so much to Doug Wald, Dominique Appel, Jason Heyman, Robert Offer, and Marc Gerald. Your belief in me from day one has meant the world to me.

Mindy Weissman, the woman who has changed my life by keeping it together. I love you.

Thank you to my mom and dad. Where do I begin? You have both believed in me since I started playing "waitress" at your dinner parties around age four. Thank you for your love and support even when you saw me making mistakes. You always believed I would find my way out and gave me strength to do so. I love you so much.

My brother, Bob—you made me strong enough to face Hollywood. And I love you so much for it. And thank you to my beautiful sister Addie and precious Nora. And to all of my family members, every one of whom is a character worthy of stardom. Loren, a special thanks to you; you gave me a gift that was much needed at a certain time in my life, and it makes me cry when I think about it. I love you.

Thank you to my son, Jack, who kicks me at night in bed. I know I will miss those nights of bedwetting one day (and you may be mad at me for writing that). But I hope one day you read just this portion and know that you light me up every day and I'm so happy and proud that you are my son. My strong, brave son.

And Chris. Chris, who, when I pitched him the idea of writing a book, didn't skip a beat. I love our late nights conjuring up ideas for projects and characters and talking about the rabbits. Chris, thank you for an impossible amount of support and love. Thank you for the flowers. Thank you for finding my credit card at the Kmart in Phoenix. Thank you for the deer jerky. Thank you for laughing at my dumb jokes. Thank you for cutting Jack's hair. But that might have to stop. Thank you for being just about the best person I know. I love you. I wish we had more words for love.